POSTER COLL

VISUAL STRATEGIES AGAINST AIDS
INTERNATIONAL AIDS PREVENTION POSTERS 06

VISUELLE STRATEGIEN GEGEN AIDS
INTERNATIONALE AIDS-PRÄVENTIONSPLAKATE

Mit einem Essay von / With an Essay by Nigel Barley

MUSEUM FÜR GESTALTUNG ZÜRICH
PLAKATSAMMLUNG/POSTER COLLECTION

LARS MÜLLER PUBLISHERS

What Have You Heard About AIDS?

What Does It Mean?

What Can We Do For People Who Have It?

How Does It Harm Us?

Can It Be Cured?

Who Can Get It?

What Causes It?

What Does It Look Like?

How Can We Stop It?

Which Of Us Has It?

Don't GUESS the Answers!
LEARN THE TRUTH ABOUT AIDS!

Adapted from the Uganda School Health Kit on AIDS Control (Item 3)
Ministry of Education, Ministry of Health (AIDS Control Programme), UNICEF Kampala

1 **Uganda**
Was weisst du über Aids? Errate nicht die Antworten!
Lerne die Wahrheit über Aids!
What have you heard about Aids? Don't guess the
answers! Learn the truth about Aids!

VORWORT

«Was weisst du über Aids?» Diese Frage auf einem Plakat aus Uganda trifft die Sache ins Herz. Denn jenen Menschen, die das Privileg hatten, Zugang zu sachlicher Information über diese Krankheit zu bekommen, konnte bewusst werden, dass «Wissen über Aids» die Voraussetzung einer wirksamen Vorbeugung ist. An der diesjährigen internationalen Aids-Konferenz wurde jedoch die erschreckende Bilanz gezogen, dass die Epidemie sich entgegen der Erwartungen weiter ausbreitet. Dem gesundheitspolitischen Auftrag der Aufklärung kommt also eine dramatische Bedeutung zu.

In den letzten Jahrzehnten hat sich in der offenen Gesellschaft der erhobene Finger staatlicher Autorität aus der medialen Öffentlichkeit zurückgezogen. Doch die Epidemie zwingt selbst jene offiziellen Stellen, die sich rühmen, einer «offenen Gesellschaft» zu dienen, dazu, sich erneut in private Belange einzumischen. Der Kampf gegen Aids hat dem Plakat seine ursprüngliche Funktion als breitenwirksames Kommunikationsmittel zurückgegeben. Doch wenn sich 20 Jahre nach den ersten bekannten Vorfällen von Aids noch nicht einmal in allen Ländern ein Konsens über die Notwendigkeit uneingeschränkter Information eingestellt hat, so kann nicht erstaunen, dass auch dort, wo eine offensivere Aufklärung im Gange ist, zumindest auf den ersten Blick, in den Plakaten höchst unterschiedliche Wege beschritten werden.

Unser Interesse galt weniger dem praktischen Ziel der Aids-Aufklärung, als der Frage, wie ihr Gegenstand rhetorisch durchdrungen wird. Mag die Zusammenstellung der Plakate aus vielen kulturell, religiös und sozial unterschiedlichen Ländern willkürlich erscheinen, so ist sie doch exemplarisch in Bezug auf die visuelle Strategie, mit der die Auftraggeber ihr Anliegen darstellen. Hat man erst die oft exotisch anmutende Oberfläche der verschiedenen Bildtraditionen durchbrochen und die dahinter liegenden Argumentationslinien freigelegt, so lassen sich über die kulturellen Grenzen hinweg erstaunliche Ähnlichkeiten erkennen – vielleicht weil das, was hier angesprochen werden muss, ans Allzumenschliche rührt: Sexualität, Krankheit und Tod.

Der Fokus des Buches legte die Entscheidung nahe, nur solche Plakate auszuwählen, die von staatlichen und anderen Stellen offiziellen Charakters als Mittel der Prävention in Auftrag gegeben wurden, weil hier ein Zwang zur Wirksamkeit des Plakats voraussetzbar war, während wir auf die künstlerischen Solidaritätsplakate verzichteten. Die als Insert behandelten Schweizer Stop-Aids-Kampagnen sollen einen beispielhaften Einblick bieten, wie sich auch auf der Zeitachse Prägnanz, Tonfall und Argument verändern oder verändern müssen. Selbst wenn alle Plakate in ihrem kulturellen Kontext erklärbar sein mögen, bleibt man bezüglich ihrer Wirksamkeit zwiespältig. Aber zu glauben, man könne dem globalen Problem in einer «globalen» Sprache beikommen, wäre naiv. Ebenso blauäugig wäre es zu denken, dass die propagierten Empfehlungen, wie der Gebrauch von Kondomen, für alle befolgbar wären. Die Kampagnen allein können die Probleme nicht lösen, doch die Bekämpfung der Ignoranz um Aids wird umsonst sein, wenn die dafür Verantwortlichen ignorant sind bezüglich Wahl und Wirkung ihrer visuellen Strategien.

Felix Studinka

FOREWORD

«What have you heard about Aids?» This question on a poster in Uganda gets right to the heart of the matter. It meant that those people who had the privilege gaining access to objective information about the immune deficiency disease also realized that you have to «know about Aids» to prevent it effectively. But this year's international Aids conference came to the appalling conclusion that the epidemic is spreading rapidly again, contrary to all expectations. So the need for health policy education acquires dramatic significance.

It is already decades since the wagging finger of state authority gradually disappeared from the public media in open societies. But this epidemic compels even official institutions that pride themselves on serving an "open society" to involve themselves in social matters again. The fight against Aids has restored the poster's original function as a broadly effective communications medium – in some countries it was only Aids that first gave it some impetus. However, twenty years since the first known cases of Aids there are still countries who do not agree that unrestricted information is necessary. It is therefore not surprising that that even when an aggressive education policy is in place a huge variety of approaches are taken by the posters, at least at a first glance.

We were less interested in the practical aims of Aids education than the question of how the subject has been treated rhetorically. This juxtaposition of posters from many countries that are so culturally, socially and religiously diverse may seem arbitrary, but in fact it is exemplary in terms of the visual strategy for conveying their ideas adopted by the institutions commissioning the posters. Once it is possible to break through the often apparently exotic surface of the various pictorial traditions to reveal the lines of argument that lie behind them, astonishing similarities can be made out beyond the cultural boundaries – perhaps also because what has to be addressed here touches on things that are all too human: sexuality, sickness and death.

The focus of this book suggested the decision to choose only those posters that were commissioned as prevention devices by state and other official institutions. In these cases we could assume a certain urgent need to make the poster effective, while not including the artistic (and thus often too self-referential) posters aimed at increasing solidarity. The Swiss Stop Aids campaigns are treated as an insert. They are intended as examples of how concision, tone and argument changed or had to change on the time axis.

Even if all the posters can be explained in their cultural context, a discordant impression is still left about their effectiveness in some cases. But it would be naïve to think that this global problem could be addressed in a "global" language. And it would be equally starry-eyed to imagine that everyone could follow recommendations like the use of condoms. The campaigns alone cannot solve the problems, but fighting ignorance about Aids will be as good as useless if the people responsible for it are ignorant about the choice and effect of their visual strategies.

Felix Studinka

2 **Vietnam**
Aids / Jugend, gib Aids keine Chance!
Aids / Young people, don't give Aids a chance!

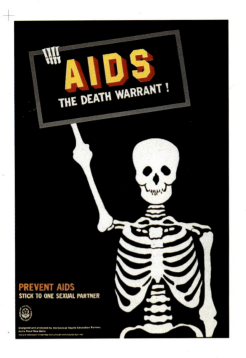

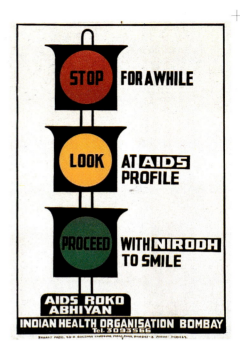

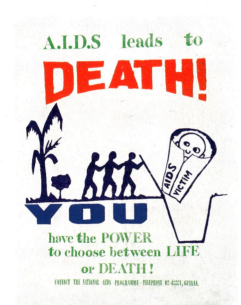

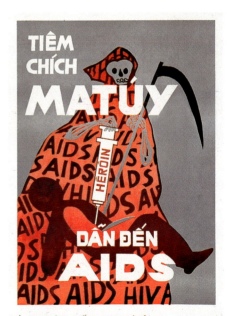

What Does A Person with AIDS Look Like?

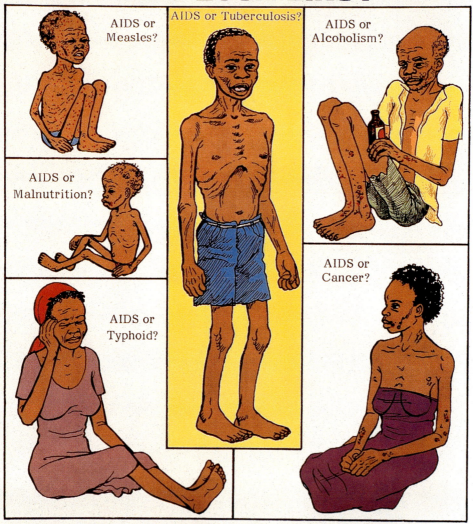

AIDS can look like many other diseases.
Don't be confused. Don't spread rumours.
See a qualified medical person for tests if you
think you or someone you know may have AIDS.

Uganda School Health Kit on AIDS Control (Item 6)
Ministry of Education, Ministry of Health (AIDS Control Programme), UNICEF Kampala

7 **Uganda**
Wie sieht jemand mit Aids aus? Aids kann wie viele
andere Krankheiten aussehen
What does a person with Aids look like? Aids can look
like many other diseases

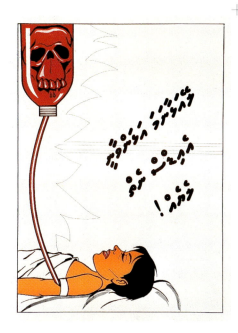

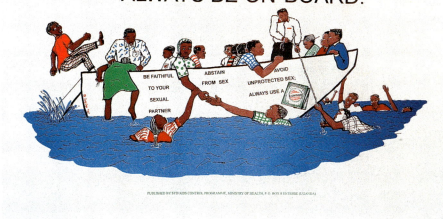

**DO NOT DROWN
IN THE AIDS FLOOD;
ALWAYS BE ON BOARD.**

PUBLISHED BY STD/AIDS CONTROL PROGRAMME, MINISTRY OF HEALTH, P. O. BOX 8 ENTEBBE (UGANDA)

8 Maldives
Machen Sie einen Aids Test / Sorgen Sie für die
Zukunft vor – Have an Aids test / Take care of the future

10 Uganda
Gehe nicht unter in der Aids-Flut; bleibe an Bord
Do not drown in the Aids flood; always be on board

9 Maldives
Wenn Sie eine Bluttransfusion erhalten, hüten Sie
sich vor dem HI-Virus!
When you have a blood transfusion, be on your
guard against the Aids virus!

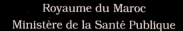 Royaume du Maroc
Ministère de la Santé Publique

المملكة المغربية
وزارة الصحة العمومية

LE SIDA

NE PARDONNE PAS
SOYONS TRES VIGILANTS

Conception & Réalisation ARTEGIS Tél : 98. 96. 73/74/75

السيدا

لا يرحم
لنكن حذرين

Avec le soutien de l' O. M. S.

بمساهمة المنظمة العالمية للصحة

11 **Morocco**
Aids kennt kein Pardon / Seien wir sehr wachsam
Aids is completely ruthless / Let's be alert

12 **Trinidad and Tobago**
Aids / Hab keine Angst / Sei wachsam
Aids / Don't be afraid / Be aware

ENDZEIT WERBUNG

Nigel Barley

Auf den ersten Blick scheint einer Publikation mit aus aller Welt zusammengetrage-
nen Plakaten zur HIV/Aids-Problematik etwas Perverses, wenn nicht gar Frivoles an-
zuhaften. Stellt eine solche Zusammenstellung nicht eine geschmacklose Umsetzung
menschlichen Elends in ein ästhetisches Erlebnis dar, eine weitere voyeuristische
Manifestation des westlichen Tourismus und seinem Appetit nach Exotischem? Doch
die Botschaften, die diese Aids-Plakate übermitteln, gehören zu den dringlichsten
unserer Zeit. Sie sprechen zu uns über kulturelle Grenzen hinweg, weil sie den zwi-
schenmenschlichen Kontakt auf der essenziellsten Ebene thematisieren – der sexuellen. Und die Nachrichten sind schlecht. In Indien und Burma ist eine epidemische
Ausbreitung zu befürchten. In Afrika steht nichts weniger als das Überleben einer
ganzen Generation auf dem Spiel. In China tritt endlich die Einsicht, dass Aids eine
grosse Bedrohung für das Land bedeutet, an die Stelle der offiziellen Leugnung dieser
Gefahr. Und im Westen sind nach einer leichten Flaute sexuell übertragbare Krankheiten wieder auf dem Vormarsch. Jede Gelegenheit, diese Botschaften möglichst
weit und eindringlich zu verbreiten, sollte mit beiden Händen ergriffen werden.

Auf der ganzen Welt spielt das Plakat in der Aids-Aufklärung eine besondere Rolle.
Es ist ein billiges und vielseitiges Medium, es kann überall ohne grossen Aufwand
produziert werden und ist optimal geeignet, um ein bestimmtes Zielpublikum anzusprechen – man braucht es nur dort anzubringen, wo dieses Publikum sich trifft. In
einer Bar erreicht man völlig andere Zielgruppen als etwa in einer Schule. Das ist
sowohl eine Stärke als auch eine Schwäche des Plakats. Für viele Menschen ist Aids
ein peinliches Thema, und während ein Liebespaar unbefangen damit umgehen mag,
fällt es Eltern oft schwer, mit ihren Kindern darüber zu sprechen. Aufklärungsaktio-
nen in Massenmedien wie dem Fernsehen bleiben daher oft wirkungslos, was bittere
Folgen haben kann. Es macht deshalb durchaus Sinn, Männer und Frauen, Kinder und
Erwachsene, homo- und heterosexuelle Menschen gesondert und in ihrer jeweils eigenen Sprache anzusprechen. Manchmal jedoch verfehlt eine Plakatkampagne ganz
einfach ihr Ziel. In Afrika habe ich zum Beispiel in einer von anglophonen Analphabe-
ten bewohnten Umgebung textlastige Plakate in französischer Sprache gesehen, die
offensichtlich nur deshalb von den zuständigen Beamten dort angebracht worden
waren, damit sie der Regierung die Erfüllung einer Zielvorgabe melden konnten. Und
viele der hier zu sehenden Plakate aus der Dritten Welt zeigen unmissverständlich,
wer aus ihnen spricht und wo ihr angestammter Platz ist: Die gebieterische Stimme
der Regierung informiert hier über Aids genauso kurz und bündig wie auf ähnlichen
Plakaten über Geburtenkontrolle oder Pockenimpfung – an den Wänden eines Kran-
kenhauses, wo die Leute sich erst dann einfinden, wenn es bereits zu spät ist 7.

Angesichts einer globalen Epidemie ist es erstaunlich, wie viele Reaktionen auf diese Gefahr ausgesprochen spezifisch für eine bestimmte Kultur und scheinbar kontra-intuitiv sind. Überblickt man die ganze Bandbreite der Plakate, ist man zunächst ein-mal darüber überrascht, dass viele derjenigen, die der bildlichen Darstellung einen höheren Stellenwert als dem Text einräumen, aus Ländern mit einer einzigen Landes-sprache und einem hohen Bildungsniveau stammen, aus Ländern also, von denen man das Gegenteil erwartet hätte. Eine bemerkenswerte Ausnahme ist Botswana, wo eine der effektivsten und phantasievollsten Aids-Aufklärungskampagnen in ganz Af-rika in Gang gesetzt wurde 32, 71. In anderen mehrsprachigen Ländern wird ein und dasselbe Plakat in verschiedenen Sprachversionen produziert 41, 42.

Auch andere stilistische Vorlieben treten deutlich zutage. In Indien und Australien werden gerne Geschichten erzählt – im Stil der aus Zeitungen, Schulbüchern und religiösen Fibeln bekannten Comicstrips 20, 116. Sie lassen sich Zeit, breiten sich aus und wollen laut gelesen, studiert und mit Freunden diskutiert werden; das, worum es darin geht, wird – vielleicht in einem Amtsgebäude oder auf einer Versammlung – unter allseitiger Zustimmung herausgearbeitet. Kulturelle Bezüge sind überreichlich vorhanden. Aids ist genauso eine Bedrohung wie die traditionellen Übel der Kinder-ehe und der übermässigen Mitgiften 33. Selbst die Götter erscheinen auf Aids-Plaka-ten. Auf einem zeigt Ganesha dem Götterboten Narada eine Schriftrolle, auf der zu lesen ist: «Bis zum Jahr 2002 werden allein in Indien 50 Millionen Menschen – das entspricht einem Mitglied aus jeder einzelnen Familie – an Aids erkrankt sein.» 14 Im früheren sowjetischen Einflussbereich herrschen noch immer die grossen Farbflä-chen und die dynamischen Umrisse der altvertrauten offiziellen marxistischen Bot-schaften vor 2, 35–37. Woanders werden diese stilistischen Mittel mit selbstbewuss-ter Ironie eingesetzt. Auf einem französischen Plakat hat eine starke Arbeiterhand ein Kondom fest im Griff: «Reprenons le préservatif.» («Greifen wir wieder zum Prä-servativ.») 59 Im Westen setzen die meisten Plakate auf eine einzelne komplexe bildliche Darstellung, um die flüchtige Aufmerksamkeit der medial übersättigten Passanten auf der Strasse oder in einer Bar zu erhaschen. Die Worte kommen später. Stil ist Kontext.

Aids ist möglicherweise die erste Krankheit, die global «vermarktet» werden muss, fast wie ein neues Produkt, das profiliert und bekannt gemacht werden soll. Minis-terien, nichtstaatliche Organisationen (NGOs) und Werbeagenturen haben sich dieser Aufgabe angenommen, und wie alle anderen Kampagnen haben auch die hier ab-gebildeten ihr Zielpublikum und ihren Wirkungsgrad, ihre Logos und ihre Slogans. Die Schweizer STOP-AIDS-Kampagne mit einem eingerollten, als «O» verwendeten Kondom als Erkennungszeichen ist darum bemüht, die Assoziation zwischen Kondo-men und Aids so unmittelbar herzustellen, dass der ganze Rest des Plakats nur noch ein raffinierter Zuckerguss ist 85. Fast unterschwellig gelangt die Botschaft ins Un-bewusste.

Bei einer Krankheit, die mit Sexualität zu tun hat, stellt sich immer wieder die Frage, was tatsächlich gezeigt werden kann, und die Antworten auf diese Frage lassen den Betrachter oft ins Grübeln geraten. Drastische Offenheit und vage Andeutungen konkurrieren um die Gunst des Publikums. Wer versucht, mit unzweideutigen visuellen Zeichen zu arbeiten, stolpert immer über das Sexuelle. In den frühen Tagen des Staates Israel wollte man der Vielsprachigkeit der Bevölkerung durch eindeutige ideographische Zeichen für alle Berufe Rechnung tragen. Ein Problem stellte der Stand der Beschneider dar. Schliesslich einigte man sich auf eine Verlegenheitslösung: das Bild eines abgeschnittenen Gänseblümchens.

Auf einer weiteren Plakatfolge der Schweizer Kampagne, die ausser dem Kondom-Logo «STOP AIDS» nur Texte wie «Wenn der Kleine gross wird» oder «Damit aus Spass nicht Ernstli wird» zeigt 99, 104, folgte fünf Jahre später eine ganze Serie von Plakaten mit hochmodernen Design-Aufnahmen «erotischer» Gemüsepflanzen 107–110. Eine grosse Distanz, gewaltige Nahaufnahmen und eine strategische Beschattung lassen diese Bilder, die zu unverblümt sein könnten, unbestimmbarer werden. Überall auf der Welt prostet man sich mit Kondomen zu, wird dieses beiläufig wie ein Kaugummi angeboten 69, in Gummistiefel und -mantel 75 und in Gummi-Shorts 74 transformiert oder mit Hilfe niedlicher Animationen 118–121 oder asketischer technischer Zeichnungen 61, 68 entschärft. Daumen 90, 95 und tadelnd erhobene Zeigefinger 16 müssen ebenso zur Präsentation herhalten wie das Washington Monument 70. Und während ein brasilianisches Plakat auf das Deckengemälde der Sixtinischen Kapelle zurückgreift und Gottvater Adam ein Kondom in die schlaffe Hand reicht 76, ist einzig und allein auf einem österreichischen Plakat ein Kondom endlich einmal dort zu sehen, wo es in Wirklichkeit wohl am ehesten hingehört – auf einem erigierten Penis 122. Nach all diesen Beispielen für verdrängten Fetischismus ist dieser Anblick in natura eine wahre Wohltat.

Wie nicht anders zu erwarten ist, sind auf den hier zusammengestellten Plakaten Darstellungen von Menschen, die tatsächlich das tun, was doch das Thema der Plakate ist, kaum zu finden. Die Botschaft, dass eine Barriere beibehalten werden muss, dass Sex «safe» gemacht werden muss, dringt in die Bilder selbst ein. Die Schweden zeigen die Staubgefässe und mit Blütenstaub bedeckten Fruchtknoten aus den peinlichen Sexualkundestunden unserer Kindheit, die auf dem steinigen Weg zur menschlichen Kopulation über das Kaninchen nicht hinauskamen 134, 135. Die Schweizer haben im Überschwang der Gefühle von den Leibern gerissene Kleider zu bieten 98, 103, die Franzosen präkoitale Zuneigung, die von Hemmungen zeugt 117. In Australien wird der ganze männliche Körper in eine Lustmaschine umgewandelt – doch nur in der sicheren Distanz des Cartoons 73. Mit unverblümten – fast lehrbuchhaft unerotischen –, intensiv beschatteten Darstellungen sexueller Praktiken zeichnet sich Österreich wiederum durch eine bemerkenswerte Drastik aus 123. Neuseeland setzt auf betörend schöne softpornographische Fotos, die einem Schwulenmagazin entnommen sein könnten 78. Viel Aufsehen erregender sind jedoch die unzweideutigen Darstellungen homosexueller Liebe 125 und die bahnbrechend offene Aufnahme zweier behinderter Schwuler beim lustvollen Vorspiel 124 aus Deutschland. Auch die Sprache zeigt merkwürdige Tendenzen. Sollte das Vokabular – auf die bildliche Darstellung abgestimmt – medizinischer, konventioneller oder erotischer Natur sein? Was besonders auffällt: Verben sind in all diesen Texten genauso selten wie Genitalien in den Bildern. In den meisten Aufschriften sind sie zugunsten guter, solider Substantive ganz weggelassen, als habe man sich an die alte englische Bühnenregel gehalten: «If it moves, it's rude.» (Obszön ist's, wenn sich was bewegt.) Und wiederum scheut das «Sei so lieb!» bittende Österreich mit «fuck» und «fanteln» vor keinem Schockeffekt zurück 123, 81, während auf deutschen Plakaten die Slangausdrücke «ficken» und «blasen» zugelassen werden 125. Einen neuen Begriff für seinen sexuellen Wortschatz wird jedoch niemand hier finden.

Unterhalb der Oberfläche wird eine fortlaufende und ergebnislos bleibende Diskussion über das geführt, was HIV/Aids aus einer kulturellen und gesellschaftlichen Perspektive betrachtet tatsächlich bedeutet. Über den Krankheitserreger und die biologischen Fakten der Übertragung scheint man sich weitgehend einig zu sein, doch die einzelnen Plakate scheinen sich nur selten mit ein und derselben Krankheit zu befassen. Während ein Plakat aus Kenia davor warnt, Aids mit Hexerei in Verbindung zu bringen 34, befasst sich eines aus Uganda gleichzeitig mit der Ähnlichkeit der Symptome zu denen anderer Krankheiten und der Tatsache, dass oft gar keine Symptome zu sehen sind 7. Ist Aids bloss eine Schwulen-Krankheit? Eine Krankheit, die nur Männer etwas angeht? Sind das eigentliche Problem nicht sexuelle Kontakte, sondern intravenös verabreichte Drogen? Ist Aids nur ein Problem junger Menschen 129? Ist man nur gefährdet, wenn man sich auf flüchtige Kontakte einlässt? Oder mit womöglich infizierten Ausländern? In Irland fühlt man sich bemüssigt, mit verdrossener Sachlichkeit zu erklären, dass selbst Iren sich infizieren können 48. Da es keinen Impfstoff gibt, versteht es sich fast von selbst, dass es keine für alle Menschen und Kulturen allgemein gültige Botschaft geben kann, und wir dürfen nicht vergessen, dass die Welt nicht unbedingt logischen Denkschritten folgt – als die effektivste Massnahme zur Geburtenkontrolle hat sich oft die Installation elektrischen Lichts erwiesen, nicht etwa der Vortrag über Empfängnisverhütung. Wir müssen uns jedoch davor hüten, uns auf moralisches Glatteis zu begeben. In Ländern mit hohen Penisbeschneidungsziffern sind die HIV-Infektionsraten um bis zu fünfzigmal niedriger als dort, wo Jungen normalerweise nicht beschnitten werden. Sollten also etwa die Organisatoren afrikanischer Kampagnen ihren Kampf gegen die weibliche Beschneidung aufgeben und sich statt dessen auf die womöglich wichtigere Frage konzentrieren, die männliche Beschneidung zu propagieren?

Wo aber liegen HIV und Aids auf der Karte der Moral? Das hängt natürlich vom jeweiligen Standpunkt ab, und es ist immer wieder aufschlussreich, nicht nur die eigentliche Aufschrift, sondern auch das Kleingedruckte am unteren Rand eines

Plakats zu lesen, um zu erfahren, wer die Kampagne finanziert hat. Auf der Aids-Bühne drängeln sich staatliche Institutionen, nichtstaatliche Organisationen, religiöse und politische Interessengruppen und Minderheitenaktionsprogramme aller Art, und viele dieser Organisationen treten offen für ihre eigenen moralischen (Zwangs-) Vorstellungen ein. Der Tradition fest verbundene Gruppen haben eine verblüffend einfache Lösung für das Problem: kein Sex vor und kein Sex ausserhalb der Ehe 19. Allein die Familienbande sind eine Gewähr für den Schutz der traditionellen Werte. Die Schweiz ist realistischer und lehnt den erhobenen Zeigefinger ab: «Du bist der Grösste. Aber nicht der Einzige» ist über einer zum Bersten gespannten Unterhose zu lesen 100, und auf einem anderen Plakat: «Das Bundesamt für Gesundheit hat keine Meinung, was das Wie betrifft, es empfiehlt lediglich das Womit.» 106 Und während für gewöhnlich die Prostituierten als Gefahr für die Freier dargestellt werden, zeigt ein deutsches Plakat einen Strichjungen mit der Aufschrift: «Du zahlst seinen Preis. Zahlt er mit seinem Leben?» 84

In vielen Ländern wird man vernünftigerweise vor die Tür gesetzt, wenn man kein Kondom benutzen will, und zieht unverrichteter Dinge davon. Wenn sich in Deutschland ein – homo- oder heterosexueller – Mann ein Kondom überstreift, dann nicht aus purer Lust, sondern aus wahrer Liebe: Wenn der junge Hans einem One-night-stand nicht widerstehen kann, dann denkt er an seinen geliebten Felix zu Hause und benutzt verantwortungsbewusst ein Kondom 77. Vom Brandmal des unmoralischen Lüstlings ist das Kondom zum höchsten Symbol für Treue und Vertrauen geworden. Und Kinder – selbst für die unerbittlichsten Moralapostel unschuldige Opfer – sind überall auf der Welt ein überzeugendes Symbol für den umkämpften Boden des hohen moralischen Anspruchs. In Thailand sind sie «das Herz der Eltern» – die einen Bluttest machen lassen, bevor sie heiraten und Kinder zeugen 24.

In der ersten Zeit nach der Entdeckung der Krankheit war so wenig über Aids bekannt, dass man glaubte, den Menschen zu ihrem eigenen Schutz nackte Angst einjagen zu müssen. Ein indisches Plakat zeigte ein Skelett, ein guyanisches ein Kinderbegräbnis und ein vietnamesisches den Sensemann 3, 4, 6. Die implizierte Botschaft war: «Was du auch treibst, hör damit auf», und das Bild des zugemauerten Ohrs, das nicht hören konnte oder wollte 58, war ein Symbol für die Öffentlichkeit dieser Zeit. Es hat jedoch den Anschein, als habe die Vernunft inzwischen den Schrecken aus dem Feld geschlagen. Viele neuere Plakate gehen in die entgegengesetzte Richtung und erklären uns, was nicht gefährlich ist 40–46. Wenn man in Österreich einen normalen Umgang mit HIV-positiven Kindern und Arbeitskollegen pflegt, ist die einzige Ansteckungsgefahr die der Menschlichkeit 25, 72. Menschen, die an Aids erkrankt sind, haben Bedürfnisse und Gefühle 128–132. In Tansania bleibt ein Freund, der Aids hat, mein Freund 127. Aids ist keine Schande, denn sogar Prominente sind nicht davor gefeit 52, und selbst Könige haben keine Scheu, betroffene Menschen zu besuchen 54.

Zwangsläufig liegen den hier vorgestellten Kampagnen zwei einander entgegengesetzte Tendenzen zugrunde: die integrierende und die ausgrenzende. Es geht also
um die Trennlinie zwischen uns und den anderen, und die hier zusammengestellten
Plakate bieten die Gelegenheit, sich eingehender mit dieser Trennlinie zu befassen.
Verschiedene Plakate heben hervor, dass Aids uns alle betrifft. Hautfarben, Alpha-
bete und Geschlechter werden bunt zusammengemischt, um eine Weltgemeinschaft
der Leidenden vor Augen zu führen. Ein Plakat aus Thailand zeigt die ökumenisch
hinter den Symbolen der Weltreligionen Schutz suchenden Völker der Erde 17. Ein indisches vermittelt scheinbar dieselbe Botschaft mit einer Aneinanderreihung religiö-
ser Architekturelemente 15, der Text appelliert jedoch an die Gläubigen, Kondome
zu benutzen, da nur diese wirksamen Schutz bieten.

Ohne Verweis auf die zahllosen kulturellen und sexuellen Praktiken, in die sie ein-
gebettet ist, und die verschiedenen Gemeinschaften, die besonders stark von ihr
betroffen sind, ist eine Krankheit wie Aids jedoch nicht zu verstehen. Oft kann aller-
dings eine schlechte Anthropologie, die es sich einfach macht und alle Schuld der
Tradition zuschiebt, schlimmer sein als gar keine Anthropologie. Ein paar Sätze aus
einem Zeitungsartikel über einen offiziellen Bericht über HIV/Aids in Irian Jaya (Indonesien) sprechen Bände: «Die hohe Geschwindigkeit der HIV-Ausbreitung ist teilweise
dem Lebensstil in Irian Jaya zuzuschreiben. Ärzten, Beamten der Gesundheitsbehör-
de und Mitarbeitern nichtstaatlicher Organisationen zufolge ist es bei den männlichen
Mitgliedern vieler dortiger Gemeinschaften üblich, ihre Frauen untereinander zu tauschen, Witwen an jüngere Brüder des Verstorbenen weiterzugeben und neue Partner-
innen zu erwerben. Ausserdem ist Sex ohne Vorspiel – was eine Verletzungsgefahr
für die Genitalien bedeutet – eine gängige Praxis.» (Jakarta Post, 30. September 2001)
Die Kultur eines Volkes wird hier der medizinischen Vernunft gegenübergestellt, die
unaufgeklärte Tradition der logisch denkenden Moderne – eine Implikation, die ganz
und gar konventionellen Denkmustern entspricht. Jedes der hier angesprochenen
Risiken wäre jedoch keines mehr, wenn alle diese Männer regelmässig ein Kondom
benutzen würden, und die völlige Zerschlagung des traditionellen Zusammenlebens
der Ehepartner – verursacht durch die Unterbringung tausender Männer in den Ar-
beitslagern des von einer ausländischen Gesellschaft betriebenen Bergwerks (das
diesen Bericht zudem in Auftrag gab) – wird mit keinem Wort erwähnt. Da sie sich auf
eine biomedizinische, individualistische Betrachtungsweise beschränken, nehmen die
Mediziner und die Mitarbeiter westlicher nichtstaatlicher Organisationen solche dem
Problem zugrunde liegenden wirtschaftlichen und gesellschaftlichen Faktoren oft
gar nicht erst wahr, und in ihren Aids-Aufklärungskampagnen sucht man sie somit
auch vergebens.

In den für die Minoritäten des Westens organisierten Kampagnen spielen kulturelle
Aspekte dagegen eine beherrschende Rolle. Wenn es um ihre Identität und die
Unterdrückung ihrer Kultur geht, sind diese Gruppen äusserst empfindlich. In den für

diese Zielgruppen bestimmten Plakaten wird daher die Gelegenheit wahrgenommen, ihr physisches und kulturelles Überleben gleichzusetzen. Gegen die Versuchungen der Drogen und des Sex werden den nordamerikanischen Indianern neben Baseball und Computern auch kulturelle Artefakte angeboten 113. In die HIV/Aids-Behandlung ist bei den Indianern tatsächlich oft auch die Fertigung solcher Objekte eingebunden – als Bestandteil der Wiedereingliederung in die Gemeinschaft, die als unabdingbar für die Heilung des Einzelnen betrachtet wird. Die jungen und sexuell aktiven Mitglieder der Gemeinschaft brauchen den Segen eines Älteren, der ihnen ein Kondom reicht 114 – vielleicht ist dieser Ältere auch ein Mensch mit zwei Seelen (ein Transvestit, dem der Tradition gemäss Heilkräfte zugeschrieben werden). Die schwarzen Amerikaner sehen sich dagegen, wenn es um Aids geht, mit ihrer Geschichte konfrontiert – die Ketten der Sklaverei sind heute die Ketten der Unwissenheit über HIV, doch der Kampf bleibt immer derselbe 115. Schwarze amerikanische Frauen werden in der vollen Farbenpracht des ostafrikanischen Kunsthandwerks für Touristen präsentiert 112, und die australischen Aborigines lehren uns, dass auch richtige Männer Aids kriegen können, nicht nur «Tunten» 116. Nur Superman-Typen wie «Condoman» sind davor gefeit 83. Auch im Stil ihrer traditionellen Malerei werden die Aborigines über Aids aufgeklärt – beschriftet wie in einer Galerie mit einer Interpretation, die flugs von einem Anthropologen verfasst worden sein könnte 111. Und Neuseeland bietet uns Maoris, die jung und schwul und sich der Aids-Gefahr bewusst sind – vor allem aber sind sie stolz: Erhobenen Hauptes präsentieren sie uns ihre schönen, mit Tätowierungen geschmückten Gesichtszüge und – unter Tiki-Amuletten und den Federmänteln der Edlen ihres Volkes – ihre wohlgeformten, muskulösen Oberkörper 136. «Wissen», verkünden sie, «macht stark.» Eine Botschaft für uns alle.

Bibliografie

M. Carocci, «'Good Medicine': Native Americans and Aids in San Francisco», *Anthropology Today,* in Vorbereitung.

A. Roberts, «'Break the Silence': Art and HIV/Aids in KwaZulu-Natal», *African Arts,* Frühjahr 2001, S. 37–49, 93–5.

R. Rowell, «Native American Stereotypes and HIV/Aids: Our Continuing Struggle for Survival», *Siecus Report* 1990, Februar/März, S. 9–15.

M. Singer und M. Weeks, «Preventing Aids in Communities of Color: An Anthropology Perspective», *Human Organization* 1996, Nr. 55, S. 488–92.

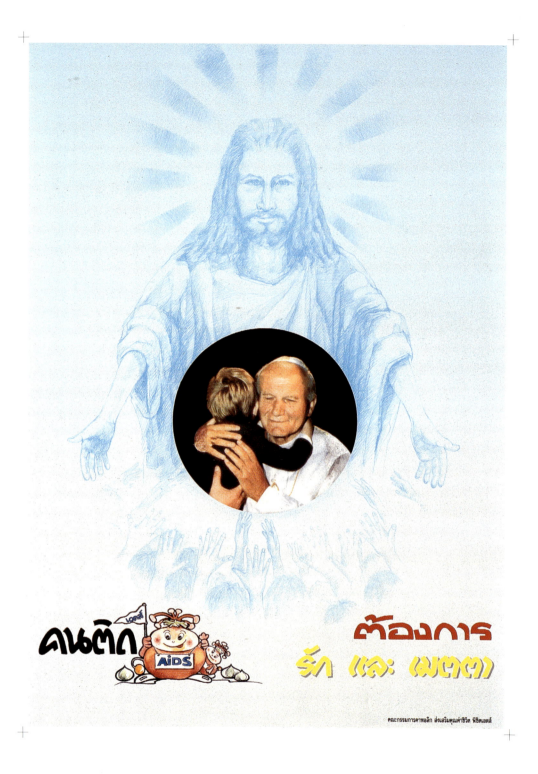

13 **Thailand**
Menschen mit Aids brauchen unsere Liebe und
unser Mitgefühl
People with Aids need our love and sympathy

14 **India**

«Geh und erzähle dem Volk offen und eindeutig: wenn
es Aids vermeiden will, soll es regelmässig Kondome
benützen»

"Go and tell the nation frankly and unambiguously
that if they want to avoid Aids they should use condoms
regularly"

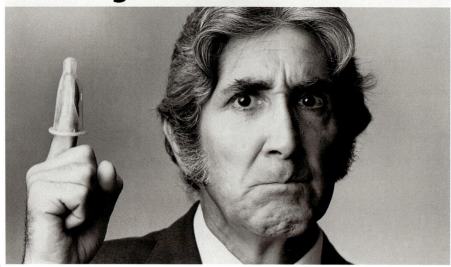

Warum erregt Aids vor allem die Tugendhaften?

15 India

Hindus, Moslems, Sikhs und Christen, alle haben ihre
falschen Vorstellungen über Aids, Bruder
Hindus, Muslims, Sikhs and Christians, all of them have
wrong-headed ideas about Aids, brother

16 Schweiz / Switzerland

Warum erregt Aids vor allem die Tugendhaften?
Why is it the virtuous who get most worked up about
Aids?

ใช้ **ศาสนา** เป็นกำบัง ยั้งภัยเอดส์

คณะกรรมการคาทอลิกส่งเสริมคุณค่าชีวิตพิชิตเอดส์

17 Thailand

Benutzen Sie die Religion als Schild, um sich vor
Aids zu schützen

Use your religion as a shield to protect yourself
against Aids

18 **Laos**

Vorsicht in der Liebe / Dann hat Aids keine Chance
Take care when in love / Then Aids won't have a chance

AIDS IS PREVENTABLE
એઈડઝ અટકાવી શકાય છે

NO SEX BEFORE MARRIAGE
લગ્ન પહેલાં સંભોગ નહી

NO SEX OUTSIDE MARRIAGE
લગ્ન બહાર સંભોગ નહી

Produced by : GAP-SIRMCE (India) B-02, Siddhachakra Appts., Pritamnagar, Ellisbridge, Ahmedabad-380 006

अनेक साथी - एड्स लावें

एक साथी - वंश बढ़ावे

19 **India**
Aids ist vermeidbar / Kein Sex vor der Ehe / Kein Sex ausserhalb der Ehe
Aids is preventable / No sex before marriage / No sex outside marriage

20 **India**
Mehrere Partner – führen zu Aids
Ein Lebenspartner – führt zu Familienzuwachs
Several partners – lead to Aids
One partner for life – leads to a bigger family

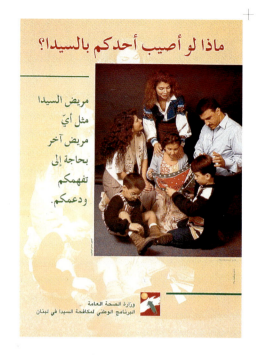

21 **USA**
Für Sie, Ihre Familie und Ihre Zukunft
For you, your family and your future

22 **Deutschland / Germany**
Verantwortung lässt sich teilen
Responsibility can be shared

23 **Lebanon**
Was wäre, wenn einer von ihnen Aids bekommen
würde? – What would happen if one of them got Aids?

24 **Thailand**
Kinder sind das Herz der Eltern
Children are the parents' heart

Menschlichkeit ist ansteckend.

Mit HIV-positiven Kindern spielen nicht.

AIDS HILFE

Wir bedanken uns herzlich für die freundliche Unterstützung bei: Gemeinde Wien, Andreas H. Bitesnich, Gewista, Druckerei Rezegh und Firma Reprodata.

25 **Österreich / Austria**
Menschlichkeit ist ansteckend. Mit HIV-positiven
Kindern spielen nicht
Humanity is infectious. Playing with HIV positive
children isn't

Natürlich / offen / Aids / Zeit zum Handeln / Aids ist eine
Krankheit, die sich vermeiden lässt
Naturally / open / Aids / Time to act / Aids is a disease
which can be prevented

27 **Uganda**
In einer Welt mit Aids leben / Auf Familien kommt es an
Living in a world with Aids / Families count and care

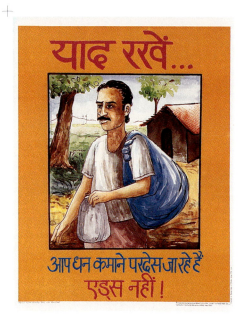

28 **India**
Du gehst ins Ausland, um Geld zu verdienen [...]
You're going abroad to earn money [...]

30 **India**
Meide die Frauen im Ausland [...]
Avoid the women abroad [...]

29 **Japan**
Gute Reise/Aber hüte dich vor Aids
Have a nice trip! But be carefull with Aids

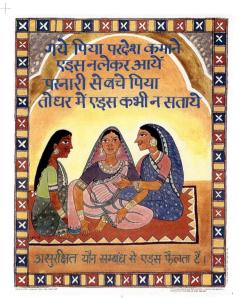

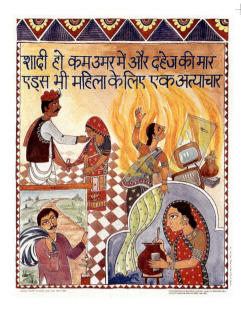

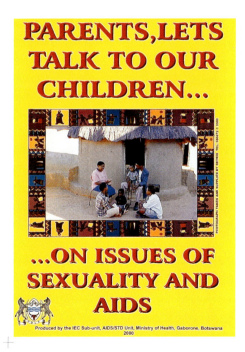

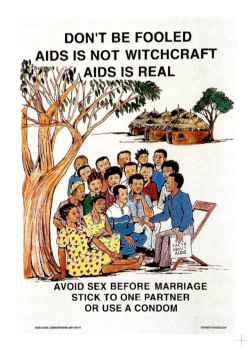

31 India
Er soll kein Aids vom Ausland mitbringen
He shouldn't bring Aids back from abroad

32 Botswana
Eltern, sprechen wir mit unseren Kindern …
Parents, let's talk to our children …

33 India
Wie eine zu frühe Heirat und die Mitgift ist auch Aids
für Frauen eine Bedrohung – Just as marrying too early
and a dowry, Aids is also a threat to women

34 Kenya
Aids ist keine Hexerei – Aids is not witchcraft

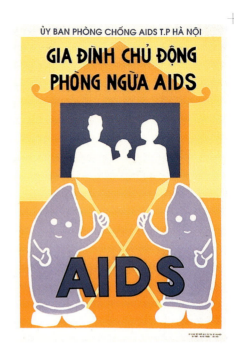

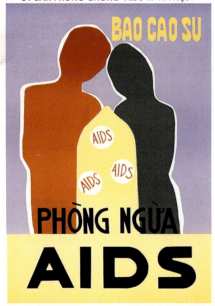

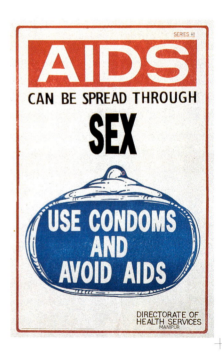

35 **Vietnam**
Aids / Keine Spritzen tauschen
Don't share needles

36 **Vietnam**
Benutzen Sie mit Ihrem Partner stets ein Kondom
Always use a condom with your partner

37 **Vietnam**
Familien, schützt Euch vor Aids
Families, protect yourselves against Aids

38 **India**
Aids kann sich über Sex verbreiten
Aids can be spread through sex

रक्त ही जीवन है

ब्लड बैंक से खून प्राप्त करने और रोगी को खून चढ़ाने से पहले यह सुनिश्चित कर लें कि खून मलेरिया, सिफलिस (गर्मी), पीलिया और एच.आई.वी. (HIV) से मुक्त है।

रक्तदान-जीवनदान

डरना नहीं समझना होगा तभी एड्स से बचना होगा

39 **India**
Blut bedeutet Leben [...] Keine Angst / Man muss verstehen, dann kann man sich vor Aids schützen
Blood means life [...] Don't be afraid / You have to
understand, then you can protect yourself against Aids

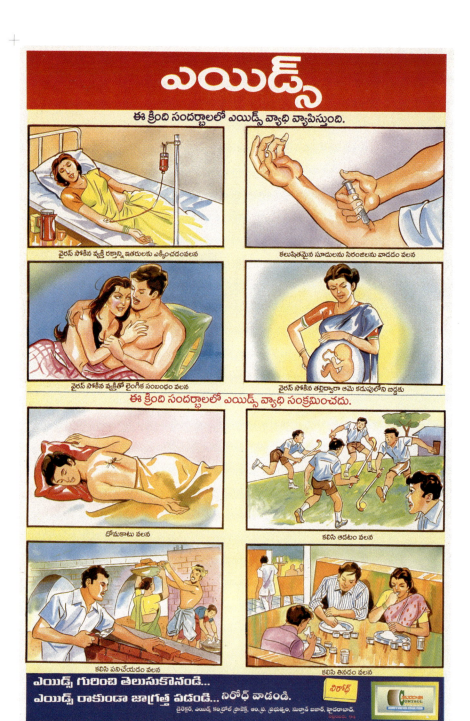

40 **India**
Aids wird so verbreitet
Aids is spread like this

AIDS HOTLINE 922-1313 (OAHU)
1-800-321-1555 (NEIGHBOR ISLANDS)

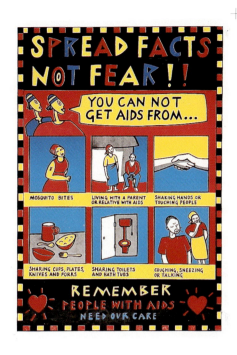

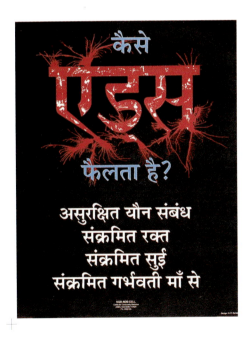

41 Cambodia
Ja oder nein / Du kannst den Aids-Virus kriegen durch
Yes or no / You can get the Aids virus from

42 India
Wie Aids sich ausbreitet
How Aids spreads

43 Zimbabwe
Verbreite Tatsachen, nicht Panik!!
Spread facts not fear!!

44 India
Weisst du, dass Aids sich nicht verbreitet über!
Did you know Aids does not spread by!

45 **India**

«Kann man Aids bekommen, wenn man gemeinsam
aus einem Napf frisst?»
"Is it possible to get Aids by eating from the same
bowl?"

46 **Schweiz/Switzerland**
Gläser tauschen/Kein Aids Risiko
Sharing glasses/No risk of Aids

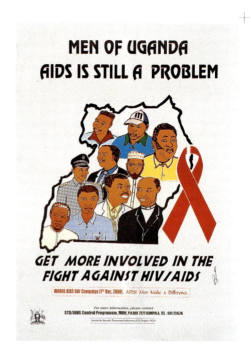

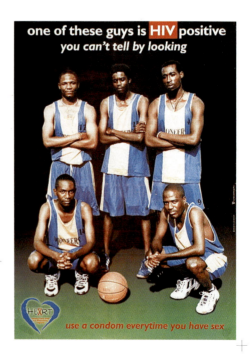

47 Laos
Aids kann jeden treffen
Aids can affect anyone

48 Ireland
Aids betrifft Iren – Aids affects Irish people

49 Uganda
Männer Ugandas / Aids ist noch immer ein Problem
Men of Uganda / Aids is still a problem

50 Zambia
Einer dieser Jungs ist HIV-positiv / Du siehst es nicht
One of these guys is HIV positive / you can't tell by looking

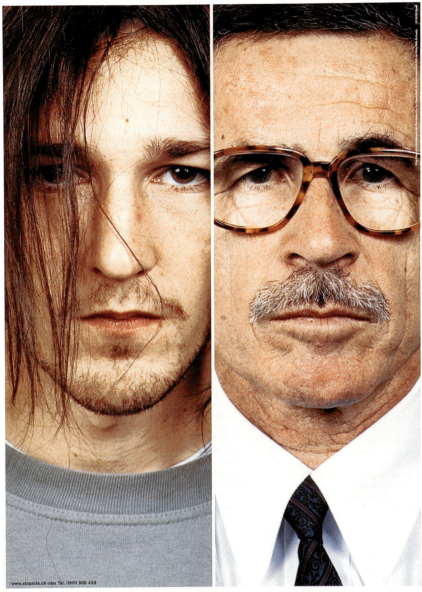

**DER LINKS HAT WAHRSCHEINLICH NICHT.
DER RECHTS HAT VIELLEICHT.**

Man sieht jemandem nicht an, ob er sich mit dem HI Virus infiziert hat. Wenn man eine neue Bekanntschaft macht,
ist es vernünftig, konsequent das Präservativ zu benutzen. Sagen Sie einfach,
es sei nicht Misstrauen, aber Sie möchten die ersten Nächte bedenkenlos geniessen können.
Schütze deinen Nächsten wie dich selbst.

STOP AIDS

51 **Schweiz / Switzerland**

Der links hat wahrscheinlich nicht. Der rechts hat
vielleicht.
The one on the left probably hasn't. The one on the
right perhaps has.

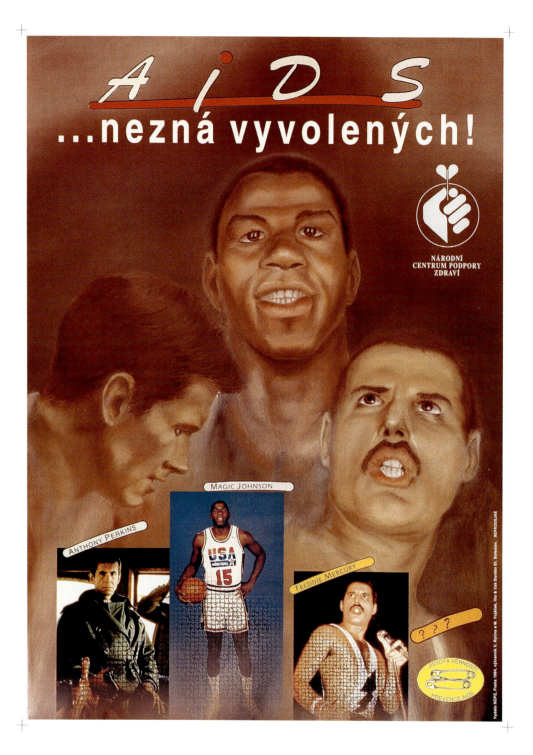

52 **Czech Republic**
Aids … kennt keine Auserwählten!
Aids … there are no chosen ones!

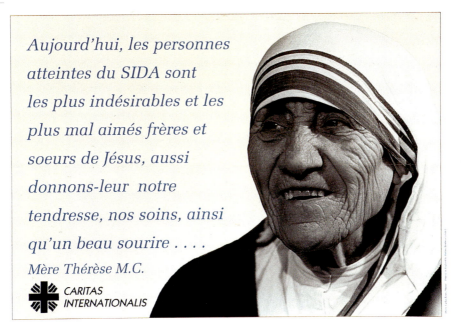

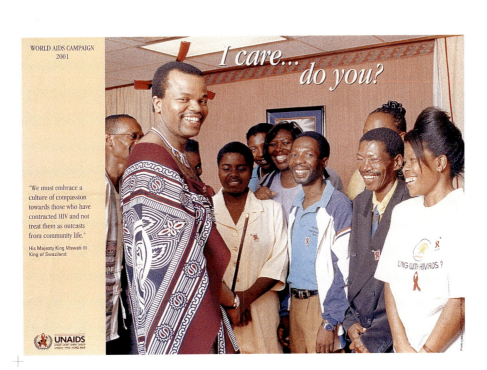

53 **Philippines**

Menschen mit Aids sind heute die am wenigsten
erwünschten und am wenigsten geliebten Schwestern
und Brüder von Jesus.
People with Aids are the most unwanted and most
unloved sisters and brothers of Jesus today.

54 **Swaziland**

Es geht mich etwas an … und dich?
I care … do you?

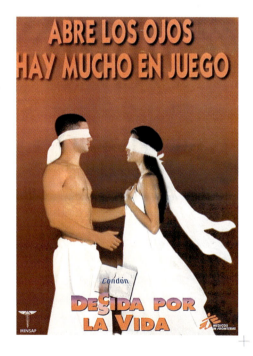

55 **Lebanon**
Nicht weghören … – Don't stop listening …

56 **Deutschland / Germany**
Wenn wir nicht mehr miteinander reden, hat Aids
schon gewonnen.
If we stop talking to each other, Aids has already won.

57 **Cuba**
Mach die Augen auf / Es steht viel auf dem Spiel
Open your eyes / There's a lot at stake

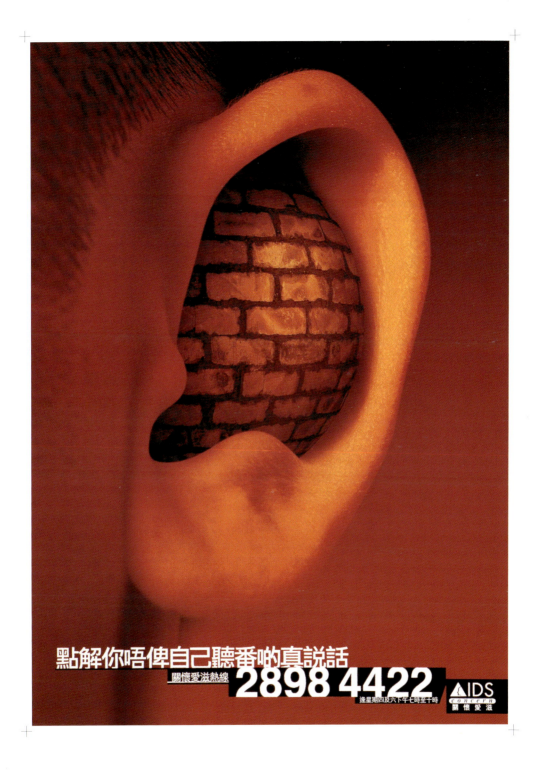

58 **Hong Kong**
Warum willst du die Wahrheit nicht hören?
Why don't you let yourself to hear the truth?

SELLING DOOMSDAY

Nigel Barley

It might, at first sight, seem perverse, even frivolous, to create a global publication of posters concerning HIV/Aids. Is this not a tasteless conversion of human misery into an aesthetic gallery experience, another voyeuristic form of tourism pandering to the appetite of the spoiled West for the exotic? But the messages crafted about Aids are among the most urgent of our time. They speak to us across cultural boundaries because they talk about human contact at the most essential level – the sexual. And the news is not good. Epidemics are predicted in India and Burma. In Africa, nothing less than the survival of a whole generation is at stake. In China, official denials are finally giving way to a sense of looming crisis. And in the West, after a slight lull, sexually transmitted diseases are on the increase again. Any opportunity to make these messages better known and better focussed should be seized with both hands.

The poster has played a special role in promoting Aids-awareness around the world. It is cheap and flexible, easy to produce locally and can target specific audiences simply by the fact of its positioning. Put it in a bar and you get one audience, a school and you get quite another. This is both a strength and a weakness. There is often an embarrassment about Aids that precludes parents and children talking about it as much as lovers do. That embarrassment can have dire consequences and make blanket coverage through media such as TV ineffective. Targeting men and women, children and adults, gay and straight, separately and in their own languages can seem like a good idea. But sometimes the aim of poster campaigns is a little off. In Africa, I have seen French posters promoting literacy programs happily distributed to illiterate anglophones to whom they were doubly meaningless, by officials only anxious to hit the targets needed for their reports. And many of the Third World posters shown here convey a firm sense that they are the authoritative, terse voice of the government disclosing serious information, in the same way they would when talking about birth control or smallpox vaccination 7. They appropriate the clinic wall as their natural home, although people turn up there only when it is already too late.

In the face of a global epidemic, it is striking how many of the responses are truly local and in ways that seem counter-intuitive. Within the entire range of posters, many of those that value image over text prove, surprisingly, to be from countries with high literacy rates and a single dominant language, where words would have seemed to be the natural medium. A notable exception is Botswana, which runs one of the most effective and imaginative Aids-awareness campaigns in the whole of Africa 32, 71. Elsewhere, the same poster may have to be produced in several different language versions 41, 42.

Other stylistic biases are clear too. India and Australia like to tell a story, using the comic-strip style familiar from newspapers, schoolbooks and religious primers 20,

116. They take their time, spread themselves and are made to be read aloud, studied, argued over with friends, their point deciphered and hammered home by social consensus, while people are waiting, perhaps, at a government office or a local meeting. Cultural references abound. Aids is as much a menace as the traditional ills of child marriage and excessive dowries 33. The gods themselves have Aids posters 14 with Ganesha showing a scroll to Narada, the divine messenger, declaring, "By the year 2002, in India alone, 50 million people – which means one member out of every single family – will have Aids." The former Soviet sphere of influence still goes for the large, flat colors and striving, dynamic silhouettes familiar from generations of official Marxist messages 2, 35–37 but this can be used with self-conscious irony elsewhere. France has a condom held in what might be called a worker's self-righteous grip: "Let us take back the condom!" 59 In the West, most posters act through a single, complex image and are designed to seize the fleeting attention of a passerby in the street or bar, already sated with a hundred contesting forms of publicity. The words come later. Style is context.

Aids is perhaps the first disease that has had to be 'marketed' globally, almost like a new product whose name and image must be made familiar and suitably profiled. Ministries, NGOs, advertising agencies have all been harnessed to the task and, as in any other campaign, those shown here have their target audiences and their degree of penetration, their logos and their slogans. The Swiss 'STOP AIDS' campaign, with its leitmotiv furled condom as an 'O', sought to make the association between condoms and Aids so immediate that all the rest of the poster was mere clever icing on the cake 85. It slips into the unconscious almost subliminally.

With a disease involving sexuality, a continuing issue is what can actually be shown, and the results often leave audiences to do quite a lot of the work themselves. Impact and inexplicitness compete and jostle each other. Typically, attempts to create a series of explicit visual signs always flounder when it comes to sex. In the early days of the state of Israel, it was decided to avoid confusion within the polyglot population by making all professions display clear ideographic signs showing just what they did. And circumcisers? They finally ended up being represented by a picture of a cut daisy.

Another Swiss series contains only lettering (e. g. "When something small gets big", "So that fun doesn't turn into a little Earnest") along with the "STOP AIDS" condom logo 99, 104. It was followed up with a range of posters showing high-fashion designer shots of erotic vegetables 107–110. Great distance, enormous close-up and strategic shadowing all lend indeterminacy to images that might be too explicit. Around the world, condoms are clinked as in toasts, passed casually like chewing-gum 69, transformed into boots and rubber mack 75, rubber shorts 74 or defused by cute animation 118–121 or austere technical drawing 61, 68. They are sported on thumbs 90, 95, reproving fingers 16 and the Washington Monument 70. And while, in Brazil, God hands limp-wristed Adam a condom from the Sistine Chapel ceiling in a clear religious message 76, only in Austria is one finally displayed where it might reasonably be encountered in the real world – on an erect penis 122. It comes as a relief to finally see one in the flesh after all this displaced fetishism.

In this collection, images of people actually having the sex that the posters are all about are inevitably scarce. The message of the need to maintain a barrier, to make sex safe, leaks into the images themselves. The Swedes show stamens and pollen-dripping pistils as in those awkward sex-instruction lessons of our childhood that got no closer to human copulation than the rabbit 134, 135. The Swiss offer exuberantly fluttering discarded clothes 98, 103 and the French pre-coital, scruples 117. Australia converts the whole male body into a pleasure machine – but only at the safely detached distance of the cartoon 73. Austria is again notably in-your-face with straightforward – almost recipe-book-unerotic – depictions of heavily shadowed sexual activity 123. New Zealand goes for glamorous images of airbrushed gay sex that could be from any glossy porn magazine targeting the same audience 78. Far more striking are Germany's depictions of fumblings and gropings 125 and the barrier-breaking frank portrayal of happy sexual foreplay between disabled gays 124. Language too is strangely slanted. Should the vocabulary, like the image, be that of the medical, the polite or the erotic body? Especially conspicuous among all the words is that verbs are as shy as genitals. Most captions leave them out entirely in favor of good, solid nouns, as if recalling that old rule of the British stage, "If it moves, it's rude." Austria, again, is deliberately shocking in flaunting both "fuck" and "fanteln", but asks us to please "be so good …" while we're at it 123, 81, and Germany has no compunctions about "ficken" and "blasen" 125. But no one's sexual vocabulary is going to be enlarged by this body of material.

Beneath the surface, a running and inconclusive debate concerns what HIV/Aids actually is from a cultural and social perspective. There may be widespread agreement about the infective agent and the biological facts of transmission but it is hard to see that these posters are dealing with the same experience of sickness. Kenya worries that Aids may be misdiagnosed as witchcraft 34 while Uganda wrestles simultaneously with the similarity of symptoms to those of other afflictions and the absence of any symptoms at all 7. Is this just a gay disease? Is it something only men have to worry about? Is the real problem not sex but intravenous drugs? Is Aids just for the young 129? Is it only a problem with casual partners? Or diseased foreigners? Ireland feels it necessary to declare with glum matter-of-factness that even the Irish can get it 48. In the absence of a vaccine, it is far from clear that there is a single appropriate message for each audience and we must not forget that the world does not move in simple straight lines – after all, the best birth-control method has often proved to be the installation of electric light, not lectures about reproduction. But we can end up in a moral maze. In countries where circumcision is common, HIV infection rates are up to 50 times lower than in other countries. Should campaigners therefore stop fighting African female circumcision and instead concentrate on the more important issue of encouraging it in men?

But where is HIV/Aids located on the moral map? Naturally, this depends on where you are standing and it is as instructive to read the small print at the bottom of a poster, saying who has paid for it, as it is to take in the headline message. All kinds of government institutions, NGOs, religious and political pressure groups and minority action programs are on the Aids bandwagon, jostling for space to wheel out their own moral obsessions. For the traditionally-minded having no sex outside and before marriage is the disarmingly simple solution to the whole problem 19 and family love is the only remedy strong enough to prevent the married from falling off the wagon of traditional values. Switzerland is less moralistic and more realistic. Lettering across a distended crotch reads: "You are the greatest but not the only one." 100 Another poster tells us, "The Ministry of Health doesn't care how you do it only what with." 106 Usually prostitutes are targeted as a risk to the client but Germany reverses the normal focus of concern by showing a posing rent boy with the caption "You pay his price. Does he pay with his life?" 84
In many countries, not using a condom means you get shown the door, sexually unshriven, and serve you right. Germans, both homo- and hetero-sexual, slip on a condom not out of lust but out of true love, so young Hans – thinking of his beloved Felix at home – always responsibly uses one on his one-night stands. 77 The condom has now been transformed from the mark of the immoral male on the prowl into the ultimate sign of fidelity and trust. And children –innocent victims even in the eyes of the most relentless moralists – are everywhere a potent symbol of the contested high moral ground. In Thailand they are "the heart of the parents" so have a blood test before getting married and having children 24.

In the early days, so little was known about Aids that fear was deployed across the board as a potent weapon to control human actions. The implied message was, "Whatever you are doing, stop it" and the image of the bricked-up, unhearing ear 58 symbolized the public attitude at the time. India shows a skeleton 3, Vietnam the Grim Reaper 6 and a poster from Guyana a child's funeral 4 – all to instill naked, unquestioning fear. But in some cases terror seems to have outstripped good sense so that many posters have now begun to tell us what is not dangerous. In Austria, normal contacts with HIV-positive children and workmates carry only the risk of seeing them as fellow human beings 25, 72. Aids sufferers also have needs and feelings 128–132 In Tanzania my friend who has Aids is still my friend 127. There is no shame in Aids: even celebrities get it 52 and kings have no qualms about coming into contact with sufferers 54.

Inevitably, two contradictory trends lie behind these campaigns. On the one hand there is the tendency to be all-inclusive. On the other hand there is an emphasis on exclusiveness, better known as the line between Us and Them and this collection offers us the chance to renegotiate that dividing-line. Several posters stress that Aids affects us all in a colorful mix of print fonts and genders to create a world community of sufferers. Thailand shows the peoples of the planet sheltering ecumenically behind symbols of the world religions all of which are under attack from the same devils [17] while India mixes religious architectures to deliver similar message but with a text asking believers to use condoms to protect themselves from Aids [15].

Of course, a disease like Aids cannot be understood without reference to the cultural and sexual practices within which it is embedded and the different communities it selectively targets. But often bad anthropology can be worse than no anthropology at all, especially when it simply shifts the blame to tradition. A few sentences from an article on an official report on HIV/Aids in Irian Jaya (Indonesia) speak volumes. "Part of the speed of transmission [of HIV] can be attributed to the Irianese way of life. Doctors, health officials and nongovernmental organization workers say that male members of many local communities practice sexual activities such as exchanging wives, passing on widows to younger brothers and acquiring new partners. Also, sex without foreplay – which can injure the genitals – is a common practice." (*Jakarta Post,* 30/9/2001) The conventional, widespread implication of this newsflash is that culture is opposed to medical good sense just as benighted tradition is to logical modernity. But there is nothing here that could not be solved by regular condom use, and no mention is made of the total disruption of traditional marital practice caused by the movement of thousands of male workers to the labor camps of the foreign mine that commissioned this report in the first place. Because of their biomedical, individualistic bias, medics and Western NGOs do not perceive such underlying economic and social factors as causal at all and therefore ignore them entirely in Aids-awareness material.

The role of culture here is precisely the reverse of that advanced in posters produced for minority groups of the West, who are extremely sensitive in matters of identity and cultural oppression. To them, Aids simply represents another opportunity to equate physical and cultural survival. To resist the temptations of drugs and sex, Native Americans are offered not only baseball and computers but also cultural artifacts [113]. In fact treatment for HIV/Aids often literally involves the making of craft objects as part of the reintegration into community that is an essential part of the healing process. The young and sexually active must have the blessing of an elder handing out a condom [114] – or perhaps that elder is actually a two spirit person (a transvestite with a traditional healing role). Meanwhile Aids confronts black Americans with the whole of history, for the chains of slavery are now the chains of ignorance about HIV, but the struggle is always the same [115]. Black American women are presented in the full-color glamour of East African tourist art [112] and Australian Aborigines teach that real men get Aids too, not just 'queenies' 116: only supermen like Condo-man escape affliction 83. Their images also adopt the style of traditional aboriginal paintings, complete with gallery label offering a full interpretation as if written by a passing anthropologist 111. In New Zealand, Maoris are gay, young, safe but above all they are proud, rippling their torsos under the feather cloaks of notables and tiki amulets or flaunting their handsome profiles complete with facial tattoos. "Strength," they declare, "comes from knowing." 136 A message for us all.

Bibliography

M. Carocci, forthcoming, "'Good Medicine': Native Americans and Aids in San Francisco", *Anthropology Today.*

A. Roberts, "'Break the Silence': Art and HIV/Aids in KwaZulu-Natal", *African Arts* spring 2001, pp. 37–49, 93–5.

R. Rowell, "Native American Stereotypes and HIV/Aids: Our Continuing Struggle for Survival", *Siecus Report* 1990, Feb/March, pp. 9–15.

M. Singer and M. Weeks, "Preventing Aids in Communities of Color: An Anthropology Perspective", *Human Organization* 1996, No. 55, pp. 488–92.

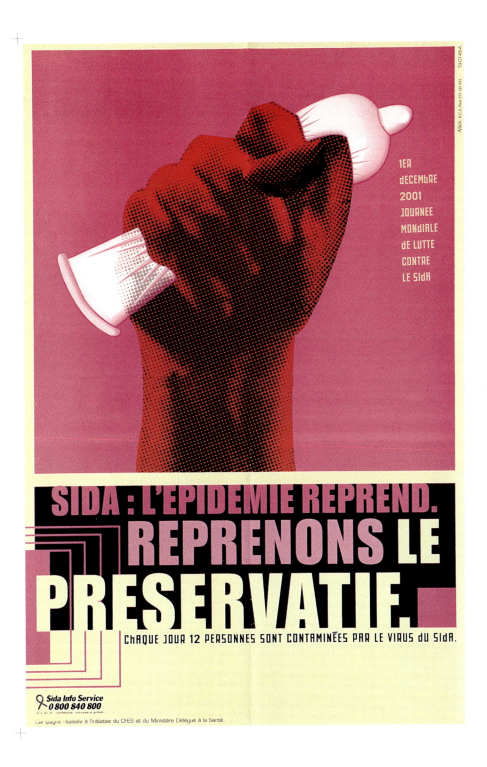

59 **France**
Aids: Die Epidemie greift wieder um sich. Greifen wir
wieder zum Präservativ.
Aids: The epidemic is striking again. Let us go back to
condoms.

Halte dich an die Technik für sicheren Sex! Verwende
Präservative
Keep to safe sex techniques! Use condoms

A AIDS PODE SER EVITADA
COM O USO CORRETO DA CAMISINHA

TIRE DO ENVELOPE.

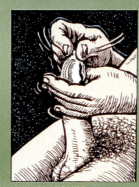

PONHA COM ELE DURO.

APERTE O BICO PARA O AR SAIR.

DESENROLE ATÉ EMBAIXO.

LUBRIFIQUE BEM.
USE PRODUTOS À BASE DE ÁGUA.

NÃO USE NADA GORDUROSO,
SENÃO ELA ARREBENTA.

TIRE AINDA DURO, SEGURANDO.

NÃO DEIXE SAIR O QUE TEM DENTRO.

JOGUE NO LIXO. USE UMA VEZ SÓ.

1º DE DEZEMBRO - DIA MUNDIAL DE LUTA CONTRA A AIDS

BEMFAM
SOCIEDADE CIVIL BEM-ESTAR FAMILIAR NO BRASIL

61 **Brazil**
Aids kann vermieden werden durch korrekten
Kondomgebrauch
Aids can be avoided by the correct use of condoms

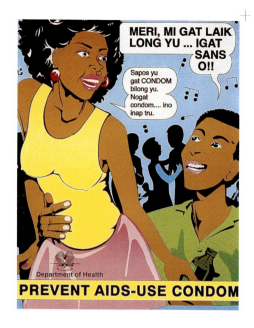

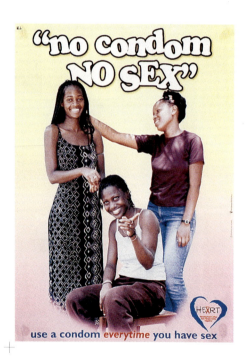

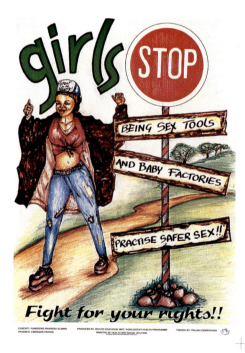

62 Netherlands
Einpacken oder abhauen! – Wrap it up or clear off!

63 Zambia
«Kein Kondom, keinen Sex» – "No condom no sex"

64 Papua New Guinea
Mary, ich hab' Lust auf dich! Sapos, hast du ein
Kondom dabei? – Mary, I fancy you! Sapos, do you
have a condom on you?

65 Swaziland
Mädchen/Seid nicht länger Sex-Objekte
Girls/Stop being sex tools

Empowerment of woman

BINDI

Bindi is the symbol of Indian womanhood. It reflects a confident, stable, dignified presence apart from adding beauty. This inspiration of confidence, stability and dignity is essential to empower woman to fight AIDS.

"EVERYTIME I WEAR A BINDI, I PLEDGE, I WILL HELP PREVENT AIDS."

Brought to you by

 HIV-AIDS INFORMATION & GUIDANCE CENTRE

WE CARE
LIONS CLUB OF BOMBAY HILLTOP

66 India
Stärkung der Frauen/«Immer wenn ich ein Bindi trage, gelobe ich gegen die Verbreitung von Aids mitzuhelfen.»
Empowerment of woman/"Everytime I wear a bindi, I pledge, I will help to prevent Aids."

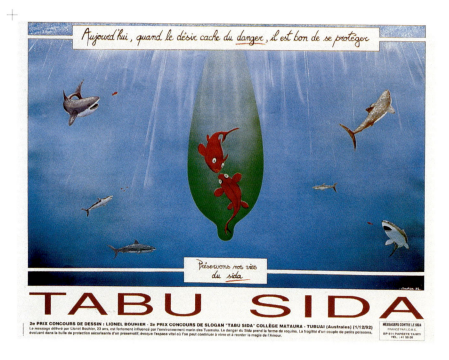

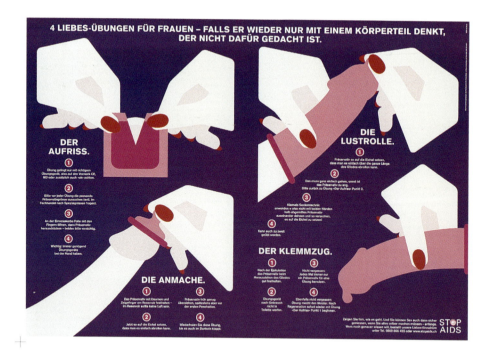

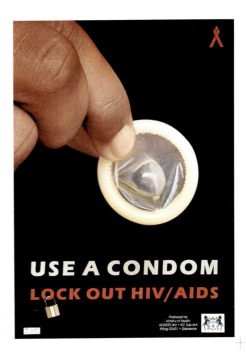

69 **Martinique**
… leidenschaftlich / aber ohne Risiko
… passionate / but without taking risks

70 **USA**
Eine Vertuschung, mit der Washington leben kann.
One cover-up Washington can live with.

71 **Botswana**
Benütze ein Kondom / Sperre HIV/Aids aus
Use a condom / Lock out HIV/Aids

72 Österreich / Austria

Menschlichkeit ist ansteckend. Mit HIV-Positiven
arbeiten nicht. – Humanity is infectious. Working with
HIV positive people isn't.

73 Australia

Minimiere das Risiko – Minimise the risk

74 Singapore

Die schicksten Kerle der Stadt tragen Gummi.
All the smartest bodies in town are wearing rubber.

75 USA

Artige Jungs tragen immer ihren Gummi.
Good boys always wear their rubbers.

76 **Brazil**
Gib auf dich acht – Take care

77 **Deutschland/Germany**
Felix schläft ruhig zu Hause. Sein Hans benutzt
Kondome. – Felix is sleeping peacefully at home. His
Hans uses condoms.

78 **New Zealand**
Sicher sein macht stark/Wir sind junge Maori, schwul
und Überlebende
Strength comes from being safe/We are young Maori,
gay and survivors

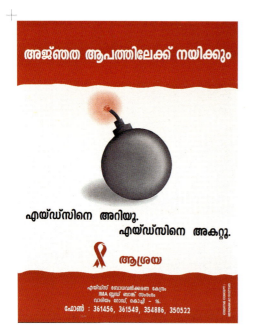

79 India

Ignoranz birgt Gefahren / Informiere dich über Aids.
Ignorance can be dangerous / Be informed about Aids.

80 Österreich / Austria

Fanteln nur mit Gummi. Kondome schützen vor Aids.
Only do it with rubber. Condoms protect you against Aids.

81 Tunisia

Stelle Fragen! … damit dir jemand antworten kann
Ask questions! … so that someone can answer you

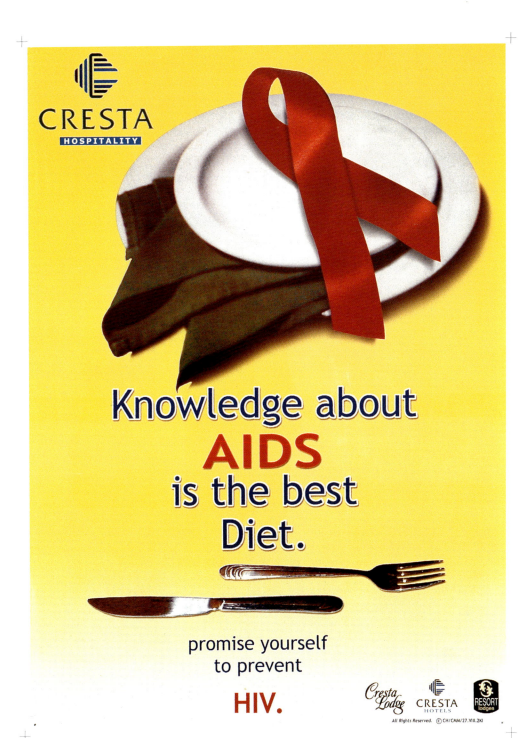

Knowledge about AIDS is the best Diet.

promise yourself to prevent

HIV.

82 **Zimbabwe**
Das Wissen über Aids ist die beste Diät.
Knowledge about Aids is the best diet.

83 **Australia**
Condoman sagt: Mach nicht schlapp, mach mit/
Benütze Kondome!
Condoman says: Don't be shame be game/Use
condoms!

Du zahlst seinen Preis.

Zahlt er mit seinem Leben?

SEX, SAFE und FAIR

84 **Deutschland / Germany**
Du zahlst seinen Preis. Zahlt er mit seinem Leben?
You're paying his price. Is he paying with his life?

STOP AIDS IN HELVETISCHER MANIER
Bettina Richter

Die Aidsprävention wurde in der Schweiz früh syste-
matisch angegangen und geniesst international Vor-
bildcharakter. Seit 1987 ist die Aids-Hilfe Schweiz (AHS)
gemeinsam mit dem Bundesamt für Gesundheit (BAG)
für die STOP-AIDS-Kampagne verantwortlich. Erstaunli-
cherweise wird diese bis heute auch von derselben Werbeagentur, der cR Basel (seit September 2001 crDDB),
gestaltet, die in ihrer Arbeit durch ein Creativteam aus
Vertretern des BAG, der AHS und externen Experten
begleitet wird. Die Kontinuität der Schweizer Präventionskampagne und der Einsatz unterschiedlicher, ziel-
gruppenspezifischer Medien sind beispielhaft. Zudem
setzte die Schweiz von Beginn an auf ein Lernmodell
und verzichtete auf das Mittel der Abschreckung. Aids
wurde auch nie dazu missbraucht, staatliche Moral zu
predigen. Die Kampagne beschränkt sich vielmehr auf
Aufklärung und Information und appelliert an die Eigen-
verantwortung. Eindeutig sind auch die ethischen Prä-
missen: keine Diskriminierung HIV-positiver oder aids-
kranker Menschen, keine Einteilung in «gute» und «böse»
Kranke. Die Aufforderung zum Kondomgebrauch als
dringlichste Schutzmassnahme wurde seit 1987 propa-
giert und findet sich in prägnanter visueller Verknap-
pung schon im Logo, das weltweit kopiert wurde.
Dennoch: Die Schwierigkeiten, ein Thema von globaler
Bedeutung, das schnellste Handlungsinitiative erfordert,
gleichzeitig aber viele Tabus berührt, wirksam in den ge-
lebten Alltag einzubringen, sind enorm. Gerade die in
der Schweiz sowohl in finanzieller als auch organisato-
rischer Hinsicht optimalen Voraussetzungen provozie-
ren daher dazu, die Plakate der STOP-AIDS-Kampagne
kritisch zu befragen.
Genügen simple Appelle, nie mit Drogen zu beginnen,
um Drogensucht zu enttabuisieren? Wo wird tatsächlich
einmal Sexualität thematisiert oder gar enttabuisiert?
Nicht das Kondom als abstraktes visuelles Motiv, sondern sein alltäglicher Einsatz im realen Leben sei Thema
der Plakatkampagnen, so die Verantwortlichen. Sind es
also diese jungen, schönen und gesunden Menschen, die
sich paarweise aneinander schmiegen, sich – scheinbar
– im Kornfeld oder im Boot lieben oder geliebt haben,
die die gelebte Sexualität des Durchschnittsschweizers
zeigen? Muss nicht schon die Bildbotschaft unmittelbar aufzeigen können, ob es um Müesli-Werbung geht
oder um Aids? Und ebenso wenig, wie ein gut ausse-
hendes Männerpaar zu besserer gesellschaftlicher Akzeptanz von Homosexualität beiträgt, wird Promiskuität
wohl wirklich zum Thema, wenn in einer der jüngsten
Kleinplakatserien, die als rein technische Anleitung den
richtigen Kondomgebrauch erläutert, das abgedrosche-
ne Klischee vom Fremdgehen des Geschäftsmannes
wiederholt wird. Ist es nicht tendenziös, wenn in der
Gesamtschau der STOP-AIDS-Plakatkampagne einzig
die Solidaritätskampagne in krassem Kontrast zum

bunten Umfeld in grobem Schwarzweiss auftritt und
ausgerechnet in dieser Serie mit Bibelzitaten operiert
wird? Ist es Zufall, dass uns hier endlich Alltagsgesich-
ter unterschiedlicher Generationen begegnen – wobei
die älteren Menschen aber nicht als sexuell aktive Le-
bensteilnehmer auftreten, sondern nur noch die Rolle
des Vorbildes wahrnehmen, das moralische Appelle an
uns richtet. Schliesslich: Wo finden sich tatsächlich einmal Krankheit und Tod thematisiert? Kann man dieses
Tabu wirklich nur in abschreckender Form behandeln?
So bleibt, auch mit Blick auf Aids-Präventionsplakate
anderer Länder, ein schaler Geschmack zurück. Zu
schön, zu glatt, zu harmlos und zu einfach ist das alles,
zu sehr dem gesamten kommerziellen Umfeld angegli-
chen. Kann es sein, dass der Zwang zum Konsens im
Creativteam zu solchen Resultaten führt?
Etwas mehr echter Witz und etwas mehr Ernst, etwas
mehr Provokation und etwas mehr authentischer Sex
täten gut – und ein gelegentlicher Wechsel der ge-
stalterischen Urheberschaft. Der offizielle Auftrag der
Information und Prävention wurde erfüllt, die Chance
aber verpasst, Fragen von gesellschaftlicher Brisanz im
Kontext von Aids aufzuwerfen. Letztlich vermitteln die
Plakate ein überaus individualistisches Weltbild: Jeder
ist sich selbst der Nächste, mit Kondomen sind wir auch
weiterhin gut drauf!

Der Umgang mit Präservativen ist einfacher als der Umgang mit AIDS.

Eine Präventionskampagne der AIDS-HILFE SCHWEIZ in Zusammenarbeit mit dem Bundesamt für Gesundheitswesen

85
Stop Aids / Der Umgang mit Präservativen ist einfacher
als der Umgang mit Aids.
Handling condoms is easier than handling Aids.
1989

86
Ok
1988

87
Nie anfangen stoppt Aids.
Not to start stops Aids.
1989

88
Schmuse/Keine Aids-Gefahr.
Snogging/No danger of Aids.
1989

89
Anna hat Aids. Wer wirft den
ersten Stein?
Ann has Aids. Who will throw the
first stone?
1990

90
Ohne? Ohne mich!
Without condom? Without me too!
1992

91
Lebensversicherung ab
50 Rappen
Life insurance from 50 cents
1989

92
Gegenseitige Treue stoppt Aids.
Mutual fidelity stops Aids.
1989

93
Mücken / Keine Aids-Gefahr.
Mosquitoes / No risk of Aids.
1989

94
Die Diskriminierung aidsbetroffener Menschen widerspricht
dem Evangelium.
Discriminating against people
with Aids contradicts the gospel.
1991

95
Ohne? Ohne mich!
Without? Without me too!
1992

96
In meiner Phantasie bin ich nicht
immer treu. Im Leben immer.
I'm not always faithful in my ima-
gination. I always am in real life.
1993

97
Wir schützen uns, weil wir uns
lieben.
We protect ourselves because we
love each other.
1994

98
«Machst du mich nochmals so
glücklich wie vorher?»
"Will you make me as happy as
last time?"
1996

99
Wenn der Kleine gross wird.
When the little one gets bigger.
1997

100
Du bist der Grösste. Aber nicht
der Einzige.
You're the biggest. But not the
only one.
1998

Wir schützen uns, weil wir uns lieben. STOP AIDS

DAMIT AUS SPASS NICHT ERNSTLI WIRD.

101
Ich war keiner Frau ewig treu.
Aber dem Präservativ schon.
I was never faithful to one woman.
But I always was to the condom.
1993

102
Wir schützen uns, weil wir uns
lieben.
We protect ourselves because we
love each other.
1994

103
«Früher haben wir nur von Liebe
geredet.»
"We used to talk about love and
nothing else."
1996

104
Damit aus Spass nicht Ernstli
wird.
So that fun doesn't turn into a
little Earnest.
1997

105
Denk mal mit dem Kopf.
Think with your head.
1998

106
Das Bundesamt für Gesundheit hat keine Meinung, was
das Wie betrifft, es empfiehlt lediglich das Womit.
The Ministry of Health doesn't have a view about how,
it just recommends what you do it with.
2000

107–110
Stop Aids
2002

STOP AIDS THE SWISS WAY
Bettina Richter

Aids prevention has been dealt with systematically in Switzerland from an early stage and this approach enjoys international recognition as a model. Aids-Hilfe Schweiz (AHS), working with the Bundesamt für Gesundheit (Ministry of Health, BAG), has been responsible for the STOP AIDS campaign since 1987. Astonishingly the campaign is still handled by the same advertising agency, cR Basel (since September 2001 crDDB), assisted by a creative team made up of representatives from BAG, AHS and external experts. The continuity of the Swiss prevention campaign and the use of different media specific to the target groups are exemplary. Switzerland also opted for a learning model from the outset, and never used deterrence as a device. Aids was also never abused for the sake of preaching state morality. The campaign prefers to restrict itself to education and information and appeals to people to take responsibility for themselves. The ethical premises are also unambiguous: no discrimination against people who are HIV positive or have full-blown Aids, no division into "good" and "bad" patients. Encouragement to use condoms as the most imperative protective measure was propagated from 1987 onwards; a compact visual version even appears in the logo, which has been copied all over the world.

And yet: this is a subject of global importance that demands ultra-rapid action but at the same time touches on a number of taboos: it is enormously difficult to introduce it into everyday life effectively. And so as the conditions in Switzerland in particular could not be bettered financially or organizationally, perhaps we should take a critical look at the STOPS AIDS campaign posters. Are simple appeals to say no to drugs enough to remove the taboos from drug addiction? Where is sexuality actually addressed, and are taboos actually being removed? Those responsible for the campaign say that it is not the condom as an abstract visual motif that is the theme of the poster campaigns, but its actual use in real life. Here we have young, attractive and healthy couples, snuggling up to each other and – apparently – making love or just having made love in a cornfield or a boat. Do they show the actual sexuality of the average Swiss person? Shouldn't the images convey immediately whether this is a muesli advertisement or an Aids prevention campaign? Surely a good-looking male couple does not really contribute to improved social acceptance of homosexuality, and equally, is promiscuity really addressed in one of the most recent poster series: it explains the correct use of condoms merely as a technical instruction, and repeats the tired old cliché of a businessman going abroad? Isn't it tendentious when in the STOP AIDS poster campaign as a whole only the solidarity campaign appears in coarse black and white, in stark contrast with its colorful surroundings, and that

in this series of all places quotations from the Bible are used? Is it a coincidence that here at last we meet everyday faces from different generations – but the older people do not seem to have a sexually active life-style, all they do is direct moral appeals at us. Finally: where are sickness and death actually addressed? Can this taboo really only be treated by deterrence and warnings?

And so, even when looking at Aids prevention posters from other countries, we are left with a stale taste in our mouths. It is all too attractive, too bland, too harmless and too simple, too much adapted to the whole commercial atmosphere around us. Can it be that the urge to find consensus within the creative team has led to these results?

We could do with a little more wit and a little more seriousness, a little more provocation and a little more real sex – and an occasional change in the design authorship. The official brief to provide information and prevention was met, but the opportunity to raise socially explosive questions in the context of Aids was missed. Ultimately the posters convey an entirely individualistic image of the world: everyone has to look after his or her own interests, and we're still pretty good with condoms.

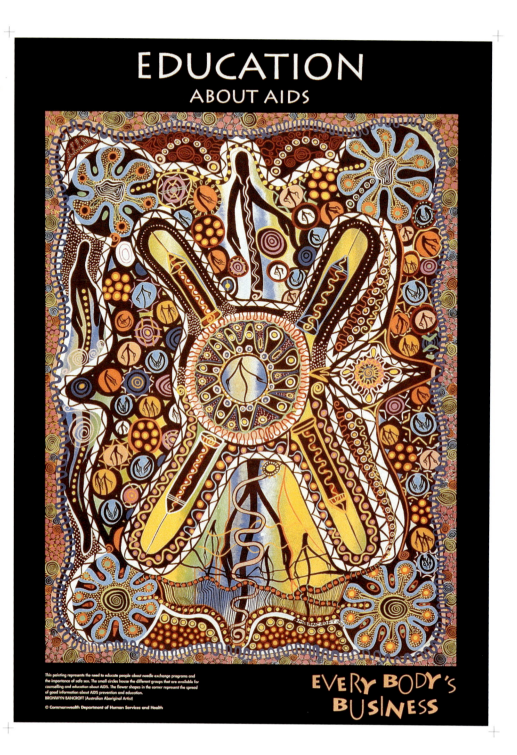

EDUCATION
ABOUT AIDS

This painting represents the need to educate people about needle exchange programs and the importance of safe sex. The small circles house the different groups that are available for counselling and education about AIDS. The flower shapes in the corner represent the spread of good information about AIDS prevention and education.
BRONWYN BANCROFT (Australian Aboriginal Artist)

© Commonwealth Department of Human Services and Health

EVERY BODY'S BUSINESS

111 **Australia**
Erziehung zum Thema Aids / Jedermanns Sache
Education about Aids / Every body's business

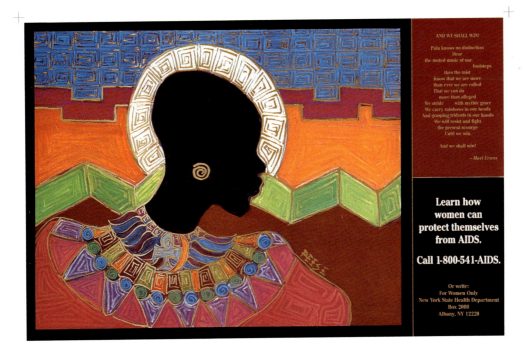

AND WE SHALL WIN!

Pain knows no distinction
Hear
the muted music of our
footsteps
thru the mist
Know that we are more
than ever we are called
That we can do
more than alleged
We stride   with mythic grace
We carry rainbows in our heads
And grasping tridents in our hands
We will resist and fight
the present scourge
Until we win

And we shall win!

~ Mari Evans

**Learn how
women can
protect themselves
from AIDS.**

Call 1-800-541-AIDS.

Or write:
For Women Only
New York State Health Department
Box 2000
Albany, NY 12220

LET'S GET OUR KIDS HOOKED ON SOMETHING...
BEFORE SOMEONE ELSE DOES.

We've got over 30 alternatives to teen pregnancy, drug/alcohol
use, acquiring AIDS and other sexually transmitted diseases...
GET WITH THE PROGRAM!

GET WITH THE PROGRAM!

SEX...BE COOL WITH IT. USE CONDOMS
AND PREVENT THE SPREAD OF AIDS.

112 **USA**
Erkundige dich, wie Frauen sich vor Aids schützen können.
Learn how women can protect themselves from Aids.

114 **USA**
Verhalte dich richtig! Sex … sei cool dabei.
Get with the Program! Sex … be cool with it.

113 **USA**
Machen wir unsere Kinder auf etwas scharf …
Let's get our kids hooked on something …

115 **USA**
Gefesselt durch die Ketten der Unwissenheit
Bound by the chains of ignorance

116 **Australia**
Du brauchst keine Tunte zu sein, um Aids zu kriegen
You don't have to be a queenie to get Aids

117 **France**
Als ob Aids zu bekommen weniger Angst machen
würde als darüber zu sprechen.
As though it would be less frightening to get Aids than
to talk about it.

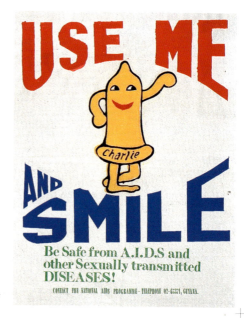

118 **Russia**
Liebe mich! Aids – Love me! Aids

119 **Bangladesh**
Geburtenkontrolle / Ausrottung von Aids / Wir sind
glücklich
Birth control / Stamping out Aids / We are happy

120 **France**
Das Präservativ? / Immer im Einsatz!!!
Condoms? Always used!!!

121 **Guyana**
Benütze mich und lächle – Use me and smile

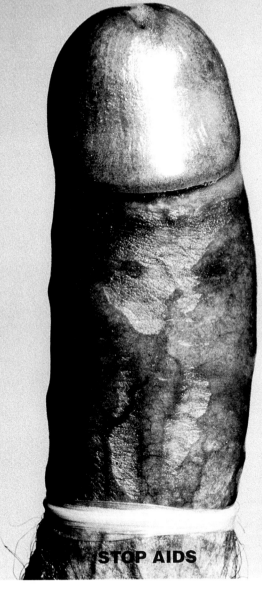

122 **Österreich / Austria**
Feiert! Stop Aids
Celebrate! Stop Aids

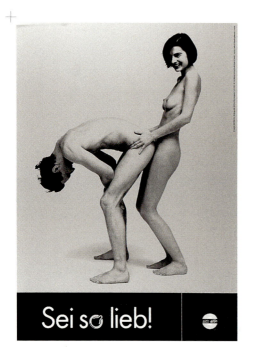

123 **Österreich/Austria**
Sei so lieb! – Be so good!

124 **Deutschland/Germany**
Selbstbewusst schwul/selbstbewusst behindert
Confidently gay/Confidently handicapped

125 **Deutschland/Germany**
Ficken mit Kondom/Küssen ist safe/Blasen ohne
Abspritzen – Fuck with a condom/Kissing is safe/
Have a blow-job but don't come

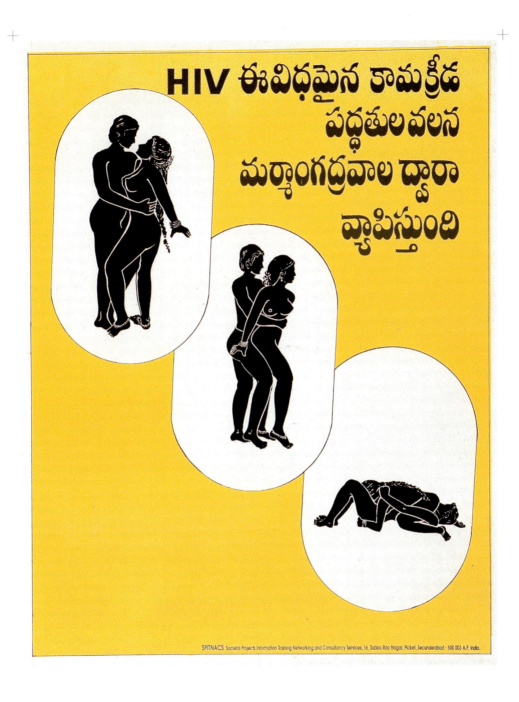

Bei dieser Art von Sex wird der HIV durch Spermien
übertragen
In this kind of sex HIV is transmitted by sperm

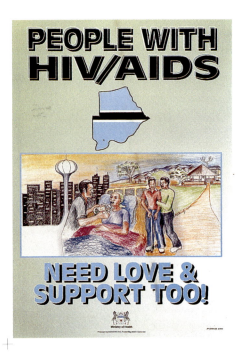

127 Tanzania

Mein Freund, der HIV-positiv ist, ist immer noch mein
Freund. – My friend with HIV is still my friend.

128 Botswana

Menschen mit HIV/Aids brauchen auch Liebe [...]
People with HIV/Aids need love & support too!

129 Luxembourg

Aber unsere Kinder und Enkelkinder sind nicht davor
geschützt. – But our children and grandchildren are
not safe from it.

130 Botswana

Kommunale Heimpflege – Community home based care

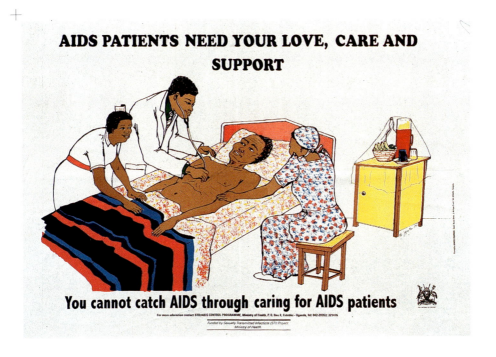

131 **Uganda**
Aids-Kranke brauchen deine Liebe, Pflege und Unterstützung – Aids patients need your love, care and support

132 **Schweiz / Switzerland**
Iris ist HIV-positiv. Wir stehen zu ihr!
Iris is HIV positive. We're standing by her!

133 **Germany**
Aids hat ein Gesicht / Du bist herausgefordert
Aids has a face / You are challenged

134 **Sweden**
Sei ein Gummi-Held / Macht der Liebe
Be a rubber hero / Love power

135 **Sweden**
Mach Liebe, nicht Aids / Macht der Liebe
Make love not Aids / Love power

strength comes **from knowing**

*being
young,
Māori,
gay and
aware*

If you are a young Māori gay/bisexual man
or a Māori man who has sex with men and
want to know more, then call:

Te Waka Āwhina Takataapui Tane
P O Box 90–256, Auckland
Phone 0–9–378 9144

**Auckland Community Outreach Centre
Māori Youth Project**
44–46 Ponsonby Road
P O Box 8875, Symonds Street
Phone 0–9–378 9802

Whakapuakitanga
Phone 0–9–309 4572

AIDS HOTLINE 0800–802 437

Photography by Albert Sword

kia tu ngā takataapui toa rangatira e

136 **New Zealand**
Wissen macht stark/wir sind junge Maori, schwul und
Überlebende
Strength comes from knowing/being young Maori, gay
and survivors

Katalog

Die abgebildeten Plakate stammen alle aus der Plakat-
sammlung des Museums für Gestaltung Zürich.
Die Daten des Katalogs folgen den Rubriken Gestaltung,
Herausgeber, Plakattext, Erscheinungsjahr, Aushangs-
land, Drucktechnik und Format. Dabei gelten folgende
Regelungen:

Gestaltung: Namen der Gestalter erscheinen nur, sofern
bekannt. Folgende Abkürzungen wurden verwendet:
A Art Direction / D Design / F Fotografie

Herausgeber: Dem Thema entsprechend ist es besonders aufschlussreich, die für die Botschaft des Plakats
verantwortlichen Herausgeber zu kennen. Die Herausgeber werden nur angegeben wo sie mit Sicherheit zu
eruieren waren. Sind die herausgebenden Institutionen
mit englischen oder deutschen Bezeichnungen auf den
Plakaten aufgeführt, wird diese Bezeichnung übernommen. Bei allen anderen Sprachen erfolgte die direkte
Übersetzung ins Deutsche.

Plakattext: Die zum Teil sehr ausführlichen Plakattexte
werden, wo immer möglich, in gesamter Länge
übernommen oder so gekürzt, dass die wesentliche
inhaltliche Botschaft erhalten bleibt. Alle nicht in
deutscher oder englischer Sprache gehaltenen Plakattexte wurden direkt ins Deutsche übersetzt. Allfällige
Umstellungen dienen der Verständlichkeit. Bei fehlender
Interpunktion trennt das Zeichen / inhaltliche Text-
einheiten.

Erscheinungsjahr: Bei vielen Plakaten konnte das
Erscheinungsjahr nicht sicher ermittelt werden, da sie
selbst die herausgebenden Institutionen in den meisten
Fällen nicht genau datieren konnten. Wir stützen
uns bei den ungefähren Datierungen auf das Jahr, in
welchem die Plakate eingetroffen sind.

Aushangsland: Als Aushangsland wird das Land
angeführt, in welchem das Plakat erstmals in den Aus-
hang gelangte.

Drucktechnik: Die englische Übersetzung der Drucktechnik erschliesst sich meist aus den deutschen
Begriffen wie Lithografie oder Offset. Hochdruck meint
relief print, Siebdruck meint silk-screen print.

Format: Die Angaben werden in der Abfolge Höhe
× Breite und in cm gemacht. Weil die Plakate oft nicht
exakt rechtwinklig geschnitten sind, werden die Ab-
messungen auf halbe cm aufgerundet.

Die Plakatgeschichte ist ein junges Forschungsgebiet
– und verlässliche Informationen sind rar.
Jeder Hinweis und jede Ergänzung sind willkommen:
plakat.sammlung@museum-gestaltung.ch

Catalogue

All the posters illustrated are from the poster collection
in the Museum für Gestaltung Zurich. The data in the
catalogue are under the headings design, publisher,
poster text, year of appearance, country of first appearance, printing technique, format. The following rules
have been applied:

Design: designer's names are only printed if they
are known. Abbreviations: A Art Direction / D Design /
F Photography

Publishers: given the nature of the subject matter, it is
particularly interesting to know who was responsible
for publishing the information on the poster. Publishers
are named only if we are certain that they have been
traced accurately. If the publishers are listed on the
poster in English or German, this information has been
included. In all other languages, the information was
translated directly into German.

Poster text: some of the texts in these posters are very
detailed. Wherever possible they have been included
in full or cut in such a way that the essential content is
retained. All texts not in German or English were
translated directly into German. Any rearrangements
that have been made are for purposes of intelligibility.
Where punctuation is missing, the sign / separates
textual units by content.

Year of appearance: it is not possible to establish the
year in which some individual posters appeared
because even the institutions that published them cannot date them accurately in most cases. Approximate
datings relate to the year in which the posters were
received.

Country of first appearance: the country listed as
the country of first appearance is the one in which the
poster was first displayed.

Printing technique: the English translation of the
printing technique is usually suggested by the German
concept, as in Lithografie or Offset.; Hochdruck means
relief print, Siebdruck means screen print.

Format: the details are given in the sequence height
× width and in cm. Because the posters are often not
cut exactly at right angles, the dimensions are rounded
off to half cm.

The history of posters is a recent field of research –
reliable information is rare. Any references or additional
material are welcome:
plakat.sammlung@museum-gestaltung.ch

1 Ministry of Education, Ministry of Health (Aids Control Programme), Unicef Kampala
Was weisst du über Aids? Errate nicht die Antworten! Lerne die Wahrheit über Aids!
What have you heard about Aids? Don't guess the answers! Learn the truth about Aids!
ca. 1993
Uganda Offset 59,5 × 42

2 Huynh Van Thuan (D)
Aids/Jugend, gib Aids keine Chance!
Aids/Young people, don't give Aids a chance!
1992
Vietnam Hochdruck 78 × 54,5

3 Central Health Education Bureau
Aids/Das Todesurteil! Vermeide Aids/Stehe zu einem Geschlechtspartner
Aids/The death warrant! Prevent Aids/Stick to one sexual partner
ca. 1988
Indien Hochdruck 73,5 × 49

4 The National Aids Programme
Aids führt zum Tod! Du hast die Macht zwischen Leben oder Tod zu wählen!
Aids leads to death! You have the power to choose between life or death!
ca. 1993
Guyana Hochdruck 56 × 43,5

5 Indian Health Organisation, IHO, Bombay
Halt ein/Beachte die Aids-Gefahren/Mach weiter mit Nirodh ohne Angst [Nirodh ist eine Präservativ-Marke]
Stop for a while/Look at Aids profile/Proceed with Nirodh to smile [Nirodh is a brand of condom]
ca. 1993
Indien Siebdruck 50,5 × 38

6 Ministerium für Gesundheit, Hanoi
Heroinkonsum und Spritzen-tausch/Aidsgefahr
Heroine use and needle-sharing/Aids risk
1995
Vietnam Hochdruck 74,5 × 52

7 Ministry of Education, Ministry of Health (Aids Control Programme), Unicef Kampala
Wie sieht jemand mit Aids aus? Aids oder Masern? [...] Aids kann wie viele andere Krankheiten

aussehen. Lass dich nicht ver-wirren. Verbreite keine Gerüchte. Gehe für Tests zu einer medizi-nischen Fachperson, wenn du oder ein Bekannter Aids haben könnte.
What does a person with Aids look like? Aids or measles? [...] Aids can look like many other diseases. Don't be confused. Don't spread rumours. See a qualified medical person for tests if you or someone you know may have Aids.
ca. 1993
Uganda Lithografie 59,5 × 42

8 Machen Sie einen Aids Test/ Sorgen Sie für die Zukunft vor
Have an Aids test/Take care of the future
ca. 1994
Malediven Siebdruck 48 × 35,5

9 Wenn Sie eine Bluttransfusion erhalten, hüten Sie sich vor dem HI-Virus!
When you have a blood transfusion, be on your guard against the Aids virus
ca. 1994
Malediven Siebdruck 48 × 35,5

10 Ministry of Education, Ministry of Health (Aids Control Programme), Unicef Kampala
Gehe nicht unter in der Aids-Flut; bleibe am Bord. Bleib treu zu deinem Geschlechtspartner/Sei enthaltsam/Vermeide unge-schützten Sex/Verwende immer ein Kondom
Do not drown in the aids flood; always be on board. Be faithfull to your sexual partner/Abstein from sex/Avoid unprotected sex/ always use a condom
1995
Uganda Lithografie 42,5 × 60,5

11 Artegis (D)
Ministère de la Santé Publique
Aids kennt kein Pardon/Seien wir sehr wachsam
Aids is completely ruthless/Let's be alert
ca. 1995
Marokko Offset 60 × 40

12 Illya Furlonge-Walker (D)
National Aids Programme
Aids/Hab keine Angst/Sei wachsam
Aids/Don't be afraid/Be aware
ca. 1994
Trinidad Tobago Siebdruck 60 × 44

13 Menschen mit Aids brauchen unsere Liebe und unser Mitgefühl

People with Aids need our love and sympathy
ca. 1996
Thailand Offset 53,5 × 37,5

14 Indian Health Organisation, IHO, Bombay
Narada zeigt eine Schriftrolle, auf der steht: «Im Jahr 2002 können in Indien allein 50 Millionen Menschen – d. h. ein Mitglied pro Familie – an Aids erkranken.» Ganesha antwortet Narada: «Darüber braucht man sich nicht zu schämen. Die Menschen sollen vom Tod verschont bleiben – geh und erzähle dem Volk offen und eindeutig: wenn es Aids vermeiden will, soll es regelmässig Kondome benützen.»
Narada is showing a scroll with the following on it: "In the year 2002, 50 million people in India alone – i. e. one member per family – could fall ill with Aids." Ganesha answers Narada: "That is nothing to be ashamed of. People should not have to die – go and tell the nation frankly and unambiguously that if they want to avoid Aids they should use condoms regularly."
ca. 1995
Indien Hochdruck 58,5 × 45,5

15 Indian Health Organization, IHO, Bombay
Hindus, Moslems, Sikhs und Christen, alle haben ihre falschen Vorstellungen über Aids, Bruder/ Die IHO versucht zu erklären, dass der Kondomgebrauch zum eigenen Vorteil ist
Hindus, Muslims, Sikhs and Christians, all of them have wrong-headed ideas about Aids, brother/ The IHO is trying to explain that using condoms is to everyone's advantage
1992
Indien Hochdruck 38,5 × 51,5

16 Warum erregt Aids vor allem die Tugendhaften?
Why is it the virtuous who get most worked up about Aids?
1988
Schweiz Offset 128 × 180

17 Catholic Commission on Aids
Benutzen Sie die Religion als Schild, um sich vor Aids zu schützen
Use your religion as a shield to protect yourself against Aids
ca. 1996
Thailand Offset 40,5 × 29

18 Vorsicht in der Liebe / Dann
hat Aids keine Chance
Take care when in love / Then Aids
won't have a chance
ca. 1992
Laos Offset 72 × 52

19 Gujarat Aids Prevention,
International Society for Research
on Civilisation, Diseases and
Environment, GAP-SIRMCE,
Ahmedabad
Aids ist vermeidbar / Kein Sex vor
der Ehe / Kein Sex ausserhalb
der Ehe
Aids is preventable / No sex before
marriage / No sex outside marriage
ca. 1994
Indien Siebdruck 55,5 × 35

20 Unesco AIDTHI, Workshop
Bihar
Mehrere Partner – führen zu Aids /
Ein Lebenspartner – führt zu
Familienzuwachs
Several partners – lead to Aids /
One partner for life – leads to
a bigger family
1995
Indien Offset 45,5 × 57,5

21 Houston Health and Human
Services
Für Sie, ihre Familie und ihre
Zukunft / Informieren Sie sich über
Aids
For you, your family and your
future / Be informed about Aids
ca. 1992
USA Siebdruck 56 × 43

22 Boek, Lauterbach (D)
Deutsche Aids-Hilfe e.V., Berlin
Verantwortung lässt sich teilen /
Vielleicht willst du alles alleine
schaffen. Aber manchmal ist es
besser, ein Stück Verantwortung
abzugeben. Um Kraft zu tanken.
Es gibt Möglichkeiten, deinen
Alltag zu organisieren, dass weder
du noch dein Kind zu kurz
kommt. Sprich mit den Mitarbeit-
erinnen der Aids-Hilfe darüber –
sie helfen dir gern.
Responsibility can be shared /
Perhaps you'd like to do everything yourself. But sometimes it's
better to give up a bit of the
responsibility. To top up your
reserves of strength. There are
ways of organizing your everyday
life so that neither you nor our
child gets less than your fair
share. Talk to the Aids-Assistance
workers about it – they'll be
pleased to help you.
ca. 1994
Deutschland Offset 84 × 59,5

23 Ministerium für Gesundheit
Was wäre, wenn einer von ihnen
Aids bekommen würde? / Ein
Aids-Kranker benötigt wie alle
anderen Kranken auch Ihr Ver-
ständnis und Ihre Unterstützung
What would happen if one of
them got Aids? Like anyone who's
ill, a person with Aids needs your
help and support.
ca. 1991
Libanon Offset 68 × 48

24 Kinder sind das Herz der
Eltern / Bewahren Sie sie vor Aids /
Machen Sie einen Bluttest,
bevor Sie heiraten und Kinder
bekommen
Children are the parents' heart /
Protect them from Aids / Have
a blood test before you marry and
have children
ca. 1996
Thailand Offset 53,5 × 37,5

25 PK & P (D)
Aids-Hilfe Österreich
Menschlichkeit ist ansteckend.
Mit HIV-positiven Kindern spielen
nicht
Humanity is infectious. Playing
with HIV positive children isn't
ca. 1995
Österreich Offset 84 × 59,5

26 Japanese Foundation for
AIDS Prevention, JFAP
Natürlich / offen / Aids / Zeit zum
Handeln / Aids ist eine Krankheit,
die sich vermeiden lässt
Naturally / open / Aids / Time to act /
Aids is a disease which can
be prevented
1991
Japan Offset 84 × 59,5

27 Claudius Ceccon (D)
United Nations Programme on
HIV / Aids, UNAIDS
In einer Welt mit Aids leben /
Auf Familien kommt es an
Living in a world with Aids /
Families count and care
ca. 2000
Uganda Offset 59,5 × 42

28 Unesco AIDTHI, Workshop
Bihar
Erinnere dich … Du gehst ins
Ausland, um Geld zu verdienen,
nicht um Aids aufzulesen
Remember … You're going abroad
to earn money, not to collect Aids
1995
Indien Offset 57,5 × 45

29 Japanese Foundation for
AIDS Prevention, JFAP
Gute Reise / Aber hüte dich vor
Aids
Have a nice trip! But be carefull
with Aids.
1991
Japan Offset 84 × 59,5

30 Unesco AIDTHI, Workshop
Bihar
Geh ins Ausland um Geld zu
verdienen und komm bald zurück /
Meide dort die Frauen, bringe
kein Aids mit
Go abroad to earn money and
come back soon / Avoid the
women there, don't bring Aids
back with you
1995
Indien Offset 45,5 × 57,5

31 S. Gosh (D)
Unesco AIDTHI, Workshop Bihar
Verdient der Mann sein Geld
im Ausland, so soll er nicht Aids
mitbringen / Hält er sich von
fremden Frauen fern, ist sein Haus
nie von Aids betroffen
If the man of the house earns his
money abroad he shouldn't bring
Aids back with him / If he keeps
away from "strange" women his
household will never have to
cope with Aids
1995
Indien Offset 57,5 × 45

32 Ministry of Health, Aids / STD
Unit, Gaborone
Eltern, sprechen wir mit unseren
Kindern … über Sex und Aids
Parents, let's talk to our children
… about issues of sexuality
and Aids
2000
Botswana Siebdruck 59 × 41,5

33 Unesco AIDTHI, Workshop
Bihar
Ebenso wie für Frauen eine zu
frühe Heirat und die Mitgift eine
Belastung darstellen, ist auch
Aids für Frauen eine Bedrohung
Just as marrying too early and
a dowry are a burden for women,
Aids is also a threat to women
1995
Indien Offset 57,5 × 45

34 Kenya AIDS NGOs
Consortium, Nairobi
Lass dich nicht täuschen / Aids ist
keine Hexerei / Aids existiert /
Vermeide Sex vor der Ehe / Bleibe
bei einem Partner oder benütze
Kondome
Don't be fooled / Aids is not

witchcraft / Aids is real / Avoid
sex before marriage / stick to one
partner or use a condom
ca. 1997
Kenia Offset 59,5 × 42,5

35 Ministerium für Gesundheit,
Hanoi
Aids / Keine Spritzen tauschen
Don't share needles
1995
Vietnam Hochdruck 75,5 × 52

36 Ministerium für Gesundheit,
Hanoi
Benutzen Sie mit Ihrem Partner
stets ein Kondom / Aids
Always use a condom with your
partner / Aids
1995
Vietnam Hochdruck 76 × 52

37 Ministerium für Gesundheit,
Hanoi
Familien, schützt Euch vor Aids
Families, protect yourselves
against Aids
ca. 1991
Vietnam Hochdruck 76 × 52

38 Directorate of Health Services,
Manipur
Aids kann sich über Sex ver-
breiten / Benütze Kondome und
vermeide Aids
Aids can be spread through sex /
Use condoms and avoid Aids
ca. 1994
Indien Hochdruck 69,5 × 43

39 Staatliches Aids-Zentrum,
Madhya Pradesh
Blut bedeutet Leben / Bevor Blut
von einer Blutbank den Kranken
verabreicht wird, wird geprüft,
ob es frei von Malaria, […] und
HIV-Erregern ist / Blut spenden –
Leben retten / Keine Angst /
Man muss verstehen, dann kann
man sich vor Aids schützen
Blood means life / Before blood is
passed to a sick person from
the blood bank, it is tested to make
sure that it is free of malaria […]
and HIV pathogens / Give blood –
save life / Don't be afraid / You
have to understand, then you can
protect yourself against Aids
1995
Indien Offset 73,5 × 48

40 Aids Control Project
Aids wird so verbreitet: Über HIV
infiziertes Blut bei Bluttrans-
fusionen / Durch die Verwendung
von Nadeln, die von Aids-Kranken
benutzt wurden […]
Aids is spread like this: through

HIV infected blood in blood
transfusions / By using needles
that Aids patients have used […]
ca. 1993
Indien Offset 88,5 × 58

41 Ja oder nein / Du kannst den
Aids-Virus kriegen durch:
Händeschütteln / Trinkbecher /
Mückenstiche / Sex / Toiletten,
Spritzentausch
Yes or no / You can get the Aids
virus from: handshakes / drinking
cups / mosquito bites / having sex /
toilet seats / sharing drug needles
ca. 1993
Kambodscha Siebdruck 51 × 40,5

42 N.R. Nanda (D)
NGO Aids Cell, Centre for
Community Medicine, New Delhi
Wie Aids sich ausbreitet / Un-
geschützter Sex / Infiziertes Blut /
Infizierte Nadeln / Über die
infizierte Mutter auf das Kind
How Aids spreads / Unprotected
sex / Infected blood / Infected
needles / From an infected mother
to a child
ca. 1991
Indien Siebdruck 57 × 43,5

43 Verbreite Tatsachen, nicht
Panik!! Du kannst kein Aids
bekommen von … Mückenstichen /
Zusammenleben mit einem
Aids-Kranken / Händeschütteln
und Berühren / Teilen von Geschirr
und Besteck / Teilen von Toiletten
und Badewannen / Schnäuzen
und Husten oder Sprechen
Spread facts not fear!! You can
not get Aids from … mosquito
bites / living with a parent or
relative with aids / shaking hands
or touching people / sharing cups,
plates, knives and forks / sharing
toilets and bath tubs / coughing,
sneezing or talking
ca. 1993
Simbabwe Siebdruck 60 × 42

44 Directorate of Advertising
& Visual Publicity (D)
Ministry of Health & Family
Welfare, National Aids Control
Organisation
Weisst du, dass Aids sich nicht
verbreitet über! Husten und
Schnäuzen / Berührungen oder
Umarmungen / öffentliche Toiletten /
öffentliche Kabinen / gemein-
sames Essen und Trinken / Mü-
ckenstiche / Du kannst dich
schützen
Did you know Aids does not
spread by! Coughs and sneezes /
Casual touch or hug / Public

toilets / Public booths / Sharing
food / drinks / Mosquito bites / You
can protect yourself
1993
Indien Siebdruck 73,5 × 48,5

45 Indian Health Organisation,
IHO, Bombay
Eine Ratte fragt die andere:
«Kann man Aids bekommen, wenn
man gemeinsam aus einem
Napf frisst?»
Die andere antwortet: «Nein,
natürlich nicht. Und auch nicht
beim Witze erzählen, umarmen,
küssen, nicht über die Kleider,
nicht über Mückenstiche, gemein-
sames Reisen und Arbeiten.»
One rat asks another: "Is it
possible to get Aids by eating
from the same bowl?" The other
answers: "No, of course not.
And you can't get it from telling
jokes, hugging, kissing, not from
the clothes, not from mosquito
bites, or travelling and working
together."
1997
Indien Hochdruck 51,5 × 38

46 Creative Realisation, cR
Werbeagentur AG Basel (D)
Bundesamt für Gesundheit, BAG
Aids-Hilfe Schweiz
Gläser tauschen / Kein Aids Risiko
Sharing glasses / No risk of Aids
1990
Schweiz Offset 128 × 90,5

47 Aids kann jeden treffen / Jeder
kann den Aids-Virus bekommen
Aids can affect anyone / Anyone
can get the Aids virus
ca. 1994
Laos Offset 53 × 37,5

48 Kieran O'Connor (D)
The Health Promotion Unit, Dept.
of Health
The Southern Health Board
Aids betrifft Iren
Aids affects Irish people
1992
Irland Offset 59,5 × 42

49 STD / Aids Control Programme,
Ministry of Health
Männer Ugandas / Aids ist noch
immer ein Problem / Setzt euch
ein im Kampf gegen HIV / Aids
Men of Uganda / Aids is still
a problem / Get more involved in
the Fight against HIV / Aids
2000
Uganda Offset 61 × 44

50 Adworks McCann-Erickson,
Lusaka (D)

The HEART (Helping Each Other
Act Responsibility Together)
Einer dieser Jungs ist HIV-positiv/
Du siehst es nicht
One of these guys is HIV positive/
you can't tell by looking
ca. 2000
Zambia Offset 41 × 30

51 Creative Realisation, cR
Werbeagentur AG Basel
Thomas Schaub (A), Marc Rutis-
hauser (D), Andri Pol (F)
Bundesamt für Gesundheit, BAG
Aids-Hilfe Schweiz
Der links hat wahrscheinlich nicht.
Der rechts hat vielleicht.
The one on the left probably
hasn't. The one on the right
perhaps has.
2000
Schweiz Offset 47 × 31

52 V. Rytina, M. Vojácek (D)
Nationales Zentrum zur
Gesundheitsförderung, Prag
Aids … kennt keine Auserwählten!
Aids … there are no chosen ones!
1994
Tschechische Republik
Offset 59,5 × 42

53 Carlos Reyes-Manzo (F)
Caritas Internationalis
Menschen mit Aids sind heute
die am wenigsten erwünschten
und am wenigsten geliebten
Schwestern und Brüder von
Jesus. Geben wir ihnen deshalb
unsere Zärtlichkeit, unsere Für-
sorge und ein schönes Lächeln
…/Mutter Theresa M.C.
People with Aids are the most
unwanted and most unloved
sisters and brothers of Jesus
today. So let us show them our
tenderness, our care and a nice
smile …/Mother Theresa M.C.
ca. 1995
Philippinen Offset 59,5 × 42,5

54 Nkomo Shadrack (F)
United Nations Programme on
HIV/Aids, UNAIDS
Es geht mich etwas an … und
dich? «Wir sollten eine Kultur
annehmen, die HIV-Positiven
Mitgefühl entgegenbringt und sie
nicht aus dem Gemeinschafts-
leben ausgrenzt.» Seine Majestät
König Mswati III König von
Swaziland
I care … do you? "We must
embrace a culture of compassion
towards those who have con-
tracted HIV and not treat them as
outcasts from community life."
His Majesty King Mswati III King

of Swaziland
2001
Swasiland Offset 42 × 59,5

55 Ministerium für Gesundheit
Aids … Und du, was denkst
du darüber? Nicht weghören/
Darüber sprechen/In die Augen
sehen – Aids … And you, what
do you think about it? Don't stop
listening/Talk about it/Look
people in the eye
ca. 1993
Libanon Offset 45,5 × 64

56 DMB&B, Hamburg (D)
Leitstelle AIDS, Hamburg
Wenn wir nicht mehr miteinander
reden, hat Aids schon gewonnen.
If we stop talking to each other,
Aids has already won.
ca. 1996
Deutschland Offset 119 × 84

57 Ministero de la Salud Pública
Mach die Augen auf/Es steht
viel auf dem Spiel/Entscheide dich
fürs Leben
Open your eyes/There's a lot at
stake/Opt for life
ca. 1997
Kuba Offset 44 × 31

58 Aids Concern, Hong Kong
Warum willst du die Wahrheit nicht
hören?
Why don't you let yourself to hear
the truth?
ca. 1995
Hongkong Offset 59,5 × 42

59 Alice. R.C.S., Paris (D)
Comité Français d'Éducation pour
la Santé, CFES
Ministerium für Gesundheit
(Ministère de l'emploi et de la
solidarité, Sécrétariat d'état à la
santé)
Aids: Die Epidemie greift wieder
um sich. Greifen wir wieder zum
Präservativ. Jeden Tag werden
12 Menschen mit dem HIV-Virus
infiziert.
Aids: The epidemic is striking
again. Let us go back to
condoms. 12 people are infected
with the HIV virus every day.
2001
Frankreich Offset 58 × 40

60 AGE Design (D)
Ministerium für Gesundheit
Halte dich an die Technik für siche-
ren Sex! Verwende Präservative
Keep to safe sex techniques!
Use condoms
ca. 2000
Russland Siebdruck 59,5 × 42

61 Ministerium für Gesundheit
Nationales Programm DST/Aids
Aids kann vermieden werden
durch korrekten Kondomgebrauch
Aids can be avoided by the
correct use of condoms
ca. 1991
Brasilien Offset 59,5 × 42

62 Projectgroep
Publiekscampagne AIDS/SOA
Ministerie van Volksgezondheid,
Welzeijn en Sport
Einpacken oder abhauen! Ich
bumse sicher oder ich bumse
nicht.
Wrap it up or clear off! I screw
safely or I don't screw at all.
ca. 1995
Niederlande Siebdruck 59,5 × 42

63 Adworks McCann-Erickson,
Lusaka (D)
Helping Each other Act
Responsibly Together, HEART
«Kein Kondom, keinen Sex»/
Benütze beim Sex immer ein
Kondom
"No condom no sex"/Use a
condom everytime you have sex
ca. 2000
Zambia Offset 42 × 30

64 Department of Health,
Australien
Mary, ich hab' Lust auf dich!
Sapos, hast du ein Kondom
dabei? Hast du keins … Ich weiss,
du bist nicht treu. Vermeide Aids
– benutze ein Kondom
Mary, I fancy you! Sapos, do you
have a condom on you? You
haven't … I know you're not faithful. Prevent Aids – use a condom
ca. 1993
Papua-Neuguinea Offset 61,5 × 48

65 Ministry of Health and
Social Welfare, MOHSW, Health
Education Unit
Mädchen/Seid nicht länger Sex-
Objekte und Babyfabriken/
Praktiziert geschützten Sex!!
Kämpft um Eure Rechte!!
Girls/Stop being sex tools and
baby factories/Practise safer sex!!
Fight for your rights!!
ca. 2000
Swasiland Offset 60 × 42

66 HIV-AIDS Information
& Guidance Centre, Bombay
Lions Club of Bombay Hilltop,
Bombay
Stärkung der Frauen/Bindi/Der
Bindi ist das Symbol der indi-
schen Frau. Er verleiht nicht nur
Schönheit, sondern widerspiegelt

ein selbstbewusstes, standfestes und würdevolles Auftreten. Diese Beseelung durch Selbstvertrauen, Standhaftigkeit und Würde ist wichtig für die Stärkung der Frauen im Kampf gegen Aids. «Immer wenn ich ein Bindi trage, gelobe ich gegen die Verbreitung von Aids mitzuhelfen.» Empowerment of woman / Bindi / Bindi is the symbol of Indian womanhood. It reflects a confident, stable, dignified presence apart from adding beauty. This inspiration of confidence, stability and dignity is essential to empower woman to fight Aids. "Everytime I wear a bindi, I pledge, I will help to prevent Aids."
ca. 1994
Indien Offset 51 × 38,5

67 Lionel Bouhier (D)
Messagers contre le Sida, Papeete
Tabu Aids / Heutzutage, wo die Lust eine Gefahr ist, ist es gut, sich zu schützen / Schützen wir unsere Leben vor Aids
Taboo Aids / Nowadays, when desire is dangerous it's good to protect ourselves / Let's protect our lives against Aids
1992
Französich Polynesien
Offset 45 × 61

68 Creative Realisation, cR Werbeagentur AG Basel
Thomas Schaub (A), Sven Kahler (D), Roger Horvath (D)
Bundesamt für Gesundheit, BAG
Aids-Hilfe Schweiz
4 Liebes-Übungen für Frauen –
Falls er wieder nur mit einem Körperteil denkt, […]
4 love exercises for women – In case he's just thinking with one part of his body again, […]
1999
Schweiz Offset 43,5 × 62

69 Patrick Josse (F)
Komitee der Aidsprävention und -kontrolle in Martinique
... leidenschaftlich, bis zum Wahnsinn ... / ... aber ohne Risiko / «Pote Chapo ...»
... passionate to the point of madness ... / ... but without taking risks / "Pote Chapo ..."
ca. 1995
Martinique Offset 30 × 40

70 Terry De Vone Wilson (A)
Roger Vilsack (A)
Mike Mitchell / Greg Snook (F)
Eine Vertuschung, mit der Washington leben kann.

One cover-up Washington can live with.
1994
USA Offset 61 × 45

71 Personalised Creations (D)
Ministry of Health, Aids / STD Unit, Gaborone
Benütze ein Kondom / Sperre HIV / Aids aus
Use a condom / Lock out HIV / Aids
ca. 2000
Botswana Offset 59,5 × 42

72 PK & P (D)
Aids-Hilfe Österreich
Menschlichkeit ist ansteckend. Mit HIV-Positiven arbeiten nicht.
Humanity is infectious. Working with HIV positive people isn't.
ca. 1995
Österreich Offset 84 × 59,5

73 David McDiarmid (D)
Aids Council of New South Wales Inc., ACON
Die einen unter uns kommen davon los, andere unter uns nicht / Wenn du das Vergnügen maximierst – minimiere das Risiko.
Some of us get out of it, some of us don't / If you are maximising pleasure – minimise the risk
ca. 1993
Australien Offset 67 × 44,5

74 Action for Aids, Singapore
Die schicksten Kerle der Stadt tragen Gummi.
All the smartest bodies in town are wearing rubber.
ca. 1994
Singapur Siebdruck 56 × 37,5

75 Turtledove Clemens, Inc., Portland, Oregon
Heather Bowen (D)
Gary Nolton (F)
Artige Jungs tragen immer ihren Gummi.
Good boys always wear their rubbers.
ca. 1992
USA Offset 56 × 36

76 4 Mars
Interdisziplinäre brasilianische Aids-Assoziation
Gib auf dich acht
Take care
ca. 1993
Brasilien Offset 62 × 92

77 Rainer Schilling (A)
Detlev Pusch (D)
Norbert Heuler (F)
Deutsche Aids-Hilfe e.V., Berlin
Hans schläft sicher bei Otto.

Felix schläft ruhig zu Hause. Sein Hans benutzt Kondome.
Hans is sleeping safely at Otto's. Felix is sleeping peacefully at home. His Hans uses condoms.
ca. 1993
Deutschland Offset 68 × 48

78 Albert Sword (F)
Auckland Community Outreach Centre, Maori Youth Project
Te Waka Awhina Takataapui Tane, Auckland
Sicher sein macht stark / Wir sind junge Maori, schwul und Überlebende
Strength comes from being safe / We are young Maori, gay and survivors
ca. 1994
Neuseeland Offset 59,5 × 42

79 Aids Bodhavalkarna Kendrum
Ignoranz birgt Gefahren / Informiere dich über Aids.
Ignorance can be dangerous / Be informed about Aids.
ca. 1996
Indien Siebdruck 57 × 43

80 Lintas AG (D)
Buenos Dias (F)
Fanteln nur mit Gummi. Kondome schützen vor Aids.
Only do it with rubber. Condoms protect you against Aids.
ca. 1995
Österreich Offset 59,5 × 84

81 Office Nationale de la famille et de la population
Stelle Fragen! ... damit dir jemand antworten kann. / Frühling der Fruchtbarkeit
Ask questions! ... so that someone can answer you. / Spring of fertility
ca. 2000
Tunesien Offset 64,5 × 48,5

82 Das Wissen über Aids ist die beste Diät.
Knowledge about Aids is the best Diet.
ca. 2000
Simbabwe Offset 59,5 × 42

83 Aboriginal Workers of Australia, Queensland
Commonwealth Department of Community Services and Health, Australian
Housing and Community Services, Queensland
Condoman sagt: Mach nicht schlapp, mach mit / Benütze Kondome!
Condoman says: Don't be shame

be game/Use condoms!
ca. 1994
Australien Offset 76 × 51

84 Alan Warran (F)
Deutsche Aids-Hilfe e.V.
Du zahlst seinen Preis. Zahlt er
mit seinem Leben? Sex, safe
und fair
You're paying his price. Is he
paying with his life? Sex, safe
and fair
ca. 1995
Deutschland Offset 68 × 48

85 Creative Realisation, cR
Werbeagentur AG Basel
Bundesamt für Gesundheit, BAK
Aids-Hilfe Schweiz
Der Umgang mit Präservativen ist
einfacher als der Umgang mit
Aids. Stop Aids
Handling condoms is easier than
handling Aids. Stop Aids
1989
Schweiz Offset 128 × 90,5

86 Creative Realisation, cR
Werbeagentur AG Basel
Jürg Schaub (A)
Hannes Huber (D)
Bundesamt für Gesundheit, BAG
Aids-Hilfe Schweiz
Ok
1988
Schweiz Offset 128 × 275

87 Creative Realisation, cR
Werbeagentur AG Basel
Jürg Schaub (A)
Hannes Huber (D)
Bundesamt für Gesundheit, BAG
Aids-Hilfe Schweiz
Nie anfangen stoppt Aids.
Not to start stops Aids.
1989
Schweiz Offset 128 × 275

88 Creative Realisation, cR
Werbeagentur AG Basel
Jürg Schaub (A)
Hannes Huber (D)
Bundesamt für Gesundheit, BAG
Aids-Hilfe Schweiz
Schmuse/Keine Aids-Gefahr.
Snogging/No danger of Aids.
1989
Schweiz Offset 128 × 275

89 Creative Realisation, cR
Werbeagentur AG Basel
Jürg Schaub (A)
Christian Vogt (F)
Bundesamt für Gesundheit, BAG
Aids-Hilfe Schweiz
Anna hat Aids. Wer wirft den
ersten Stein?
Ann has Aids. Who will throw the

first stone?
1990
Schweiz Offset 128 × 275

90 Creative Realisation, cR
Werbeagentur AG Basel
Thomas Schaub (A)
Hannes Huber (D)
Markus Rössle (F)
Bundesamt für Gesundheit, BAG
Aids-Hilfe Schweiz
Ohne? Ohne mich!
Without condom? Without me
too!
1992
Schweiz Offset 128 × 275

91 Creative Realisation, cR
Werbeagentur AG Basel
Jürg Schaub (A)
Hannes Huber (D)
Bundesamt für Gesundheit, BAG
Lebensversicherung ab
50 Rappen
Life insurance from 50 cents
1989
Schweiz Offset 128 × 275

92 Creative Realisation, cR
Werbeagentur AG Basel
Jürg Schaub (A)
Hannes Huber (D)
Bundesamt für Gesundheit, BAG
Aids-Hilfe Schweiz
Gegenseitige Treue stoppt Aids.
Mutual fidelity stops Aids.
1989
Schweiz Offset 128 × 275

93 Creative Realisation, cR
Werbeagentur AG Basel
Jürg Schaub (A)
Hannes Huber (D)
Bundesamt für Gesundheit, BAG
Aids-Hilfe Schweiz
Mücken/Keine Aids-Gefahr.
Mosquitoes/No risk of Aids.
1989
Schweiz Offset 128 × 275

94 Creative Realisation, cR
Werbeagentur AG Basel
Jürg Schaub (A)
Christian Vogt (F)
Bundesamt für Gesundheit, BAG
Aids-Hilfe Schweiz
Kardinal Heinrich Schwery,
Bischof von Sitten/Die
Diskriminierung aidsbetroffener
Menschen widerspricht dem
Evangelium.
Cardinal Heinrich Schwery,
Bishop of Sitten/Discriminating
against people with Aids
contradicts the gospel.
1991
Schweiz Offset 128 × 275

95 Creative Realisation, cR
Werbeagentur AG Basel
Thomas Schaub (A)
Hannes Huber (D)
Markus Rössle (F)
Bundesamt für Gesundheit, BAG
Aids-Hilfe Schweiz
Ohne? Ohne mich!
Without? Without me too!
1992
Schweiz Offset 128 × 275

96 Creative Realisation, cR
Werbeagentur AG Basel
Thomas Schaub (A)
Hannes Huber (D)
Adriano Biondo (F)
Bundesamt für Gesundheit, BAG
Aids-Hilfe Schweiz
In meiner Phantasie bin ich nicht
immer treu. Im Leben immer.
I'm not always faithful in my imag-
ination. I always am in real life.
1993
Schweiz Offset 128 × 275

97 Creative Realisation, cR
Werbeagentur AG Basel
Thomas Schaub (A)
Markus Rössle (F)
Bundesamt für Gesundheit, BAG
Aids-Hilfe Schweiz
Wir schützen uns, weil wir uns
lieben.
We protect ourselves because we
love each other.
1994
Schweiz Offset 128 × 275

98 Creative Realisation, cR
Werbeagentur AG Basel
Thomas Schaub (A)
Bundesamt für Gesundheit, BAG
Aids-Hilfe Schweiz
«Machst du mich nochmals
so glücklich wie vorher?» Das
Präservativ. Immer dabei.
"Will you make me as happy as
last time?" The condom. Always
there.
1996
Schweiz Offset 128 × 275

99 Creative Realisation, cR
Werbeagentur AG Basel
Thomas Schaub (A)
Bundesamt für Gesundheit, BAG
Aids-Hilfe Schweiz
Wenn der Kleine gross wird.
Präservative bieten Sicherheit für
alle.
When the little one gets bigger.
Condoms offer safety for all.
1997
Schweiz Offset 128 × 275

100 Creative Realisation, cR
Werbeagentur AG Basel

Thomas Schaub (A)
Markus Rössle (F)
Bundesamt für Gesundheit, BAG
Aids-Hilfe Schweiz
Du bist der Grösste. Aber nicht
der Einzige. Kein Seitensprung
ohne Präservativ.
You're the biggest. But not the
only one. No infidelity without a
condom.
1998
Schweiz Offset 128 × 275

101 Creative Realisation, cR
Werbeagentur AG Basel
Thomas Schaub (A)
Hannes Huber (D)
Adriano Biondo (F)
Bundesamt für Gesundheit, BAG
Aids-Hilfe Schweiz
Ich war keiner Frau ewig treu.
Aber dem Präservativ schon.
I was never faithful to one woman.
But I always was to the condom.
1993
Schweiz Offset 128 × 275

102 Creative Realisation, cR
Werbeagentur AG Basel
Thomas Schaub (A)
Markus Rössle (F)
Bundesamt für Gesundheit, BAG
Aids-Hilfe Schweiz
Wir schützen uns, weil wir uns
lieben.
We protect ourselves because we
love each other.
1994
Schweiz Offset 128 × 275

103 Creative Realisation, cR
Werbeagentur AG Basel
Thomas Schaub (A)
Bundesamt für Gesundheit, BAG
Aids-Hilfe Schweiz
«Früher haben wir nur von Liebe
geredet.» Das Präservativ. Immer
dabei.
"We used to talk about love and
nothing else." The condom.
Always there.
1996
Schweiz Offset 128 × 275

104 Creative Realisation, cR
Werbeagentur AG Basel
Thomas Schaub (A)
Bundesamt für Gesundheit, BAG
Aids-Hilfe Schweiz
Damit aus Spass nicht Ernstli
wird. Präservative bieten Sicher-
heit für alle.
So that fun doesn't turn into
a little Earnest. Condoms offer
safety for everyone.
1997
Schweiz Offset 128 × 275

105 Creative Realisation, cR
Werbeagentur AG Basel
Thomas Schaub (A)
Markus Rössle (F)
Bundesamt für Gesundheit, BAG
Aids-Hilfe Schweiz
Denk mal mit dem Kopf. Kein
Seitensprung ohne Präservativ.
Think with your head. No infidelity
without a condom.
1998
Schweiz Offset 128 × 275

106 Creative Realisation, cR
Werbeagentur AG Basel
Thomas Schaub (A), Roger
Horvath (D)
Andri Pol (F)
Bundesamt für Gesundheit, BAG
Aids-Hilfe Schweiz
Das Bundesamt für Gesundheit
hat keine Meinung, was das
Wie betrifft, es empfiehlt lediglich
das Womit.
The Ministry of Health doesn't
have a view about how, it just
recommends what you do it with.
2000
Schweiz Offset 47 × 31

107–110 crDDB Basel
Michael Oswald (A), Michael
Oswald, Marc Rutishauser (D)
Harry Burst (F)
Bundesamt für Gesundheit, BAG
Aids-Hilfe Schweiz
Stop Aids
2002
Schweiz Offset 50 × 110

111 Bronwyn Bancroft (D)
Commonwealth Department of
Community Services and Health
Erziehung zum Thema Aids/
Jedermanns Sache
Education about Aids/Every
body's business
1992
Australien Offset 89 × 61

112 New York State Health
Department
Erkundige dich, wie Frauen sich
vor Aids schützen können.
Learn how women can protect
themselves from Aids.
ca. 1994
USA Offset 35 × 55

113 Christine Salvador (D)
Stewart Tilger (F)
Seattle Indian Health Board
Machen wir unsere Kinder
auf etwas scharf … bevor dies ein
anderer tut. Wir haben mehr als
30 Alternativen zu Schwanger-
schaft von Minderjährigen,
Alkohol- oder Drogenmissbrauch,

Ansteckung mit Aids oder
anderen Geschlechtskrankheiten
… Verhalte dich richtig!
Let' get our kids hooked on
something … before someone
else does. We've got over 30
alternatives to teen pregnancy,
drug/alcohol use, acquiring Aids
and other sexually transmitted
diseases … Get with the program!
ca. 1993
USA Offset 58 × 44

114 Christine Salvador (D)
Stewart Tilger (F)
Seattle Indian Health Board
Verhalte dich richtig! Sex …
sei cool dabei. Benütze Kondome
und verhindere die Verbreitung
von Aids.
Get with the Program! Sex …
be cool with it. Use Condoms and
prevent the spread of Aids.
ca. 1993
USA Offset 58 × 44

115 Deborah Riley (D)
S.C. Aids Education Network Inc.
S.C. Coalition of black church
leaders Inc.
Gefesselt durch die Ketten der
Unwissenheit/Informiere dich
über Aids
Bound by the chains of ignorance/
Learn about Aids
ca. 1994
USA Offset 61 × 46

116 Commonwealth Department
of Community Services and
Health, Queensland
Du brauchst keine Tunte zu sein,
um Aids zu kriegen
You don't have to be a queenie to
get Aids
ca. 1995
Australien Offset 51 × 76

117 Euro RSCG, Nanterre (D)
Comité Français d'Éducation pour
la Santé, CFES
Eine neue Geschichte, zwischen
Ihnen funkt's. Wenn Sie ihm
jetzt mit Präservativen kommen,
befürchten Sie, alles zu verderben
und für ein Mädchen durchzu-
gehen, das nur an das Eine denkt.
Als ob Aids zu bekommen
weniger Angst machen würde als
darüber zu sprechen.
Here we go, those two have
clicked. If you start on at him about
condoms now you'll be afraid
of spoiling everything and going
through all that just for a girl
who's only got one thought in
her head. As though it would be
less frightening to get Aids than

to talk about it.
ca. 1996
Frankreich Offset 40 × 60

118 I.P. Gurov (D)
Republikanisches Zentrum für
medizinische Prophylaxe
Liebe mich! Aids
Love me! Aids
1993
Russland Siebdruck 58 × 41

119 Geburtenkontrolle /
Ausrottung von Aids / Wir sind
glücklich
Birth control. Stamping out Aids /
We are happy
ca. 1991
Bangladesch Offset 75 × 49

120 Les élèves du Lycée Léo
Lagrange, Bondy (D)
Centres Régionaux d'Informations
et de Prévention du Sida, CRIPS
Das Präservativ? / Immer im
Einsatz!!!
Condoms? Always used!!!
2001
Frankreich Offset 42 × 30

121 The National Aids Programme
Benütze mich und lächle /
Charlie / Schütze dich vor Aids und
anderen sexuell übertragbaren
Krankheiten!
Use me and smile / Charlie / Be
safe from A.I.D.S and other
sexually transmitted diseases!
ca. 1993
Guyana Hochdruck 56 × 43,5

122 Matthias Herrmann / Grazer
Kunstverein (D)
Steirische Aids-Hilfe
Feiert! Stop Aids
Celebrate! Stop Aids
1993
Österreich Offset 84 × 59,5

123 Andreas Pawlik, Florian
Pumhösl (D)
Matthias Herrmann (F)
Aids-Hilfe Wien
Sei so lieb!
Be so good!
ca. 1993
Österreich Offset 84 × 60

124 Wolfgang Mudra (D)
Ines de Nil (F)
Deutsche Aids-Hilfe e.V.
Selbstbewusst schwul / selbstbe-
wusst behindert
Confidently gay / Confidently
handicapped
ca. 1995
Deutschland Offset 68 × 48

125 Wolfgang Mudra (D)
Michael Taubenheim (F)
Deutsche Aids-Hilfe e.V.
Ficken mit Kondom / Küssen ist
safe / Blasen ohne Abspritzen
Fuck with a condom / Kissing is
safe / Have a blow-job but don't
come
ca. 1993
Deutschland Offset 59,5 × 84

126 Societal Projects Information
Training Networking and
Consultancy Services, SPITNACS
Bei dieser Art von Sex wird der
HIV durch Spermien übertragen
In this kind of sex HIV is trans-
mitted by sperm
ca. 1995
Indien Siebdruck 57 × 44,5

127 Marco Tibasima (D)
Center for Sexual Health
Mein Freund, der HIV-positiv ist,
ist immer noch mein Freund.
My friend with HIV is still my
friend.
ca. 1994
Tansania Offset 60,5 × 46

128 Ministry of Health, Aids / STD
Unit, Gaborone
Menschen mit HIV / Aids brauchen
auch Liebe und Unterstützung!
People with HIV / Aids need love
& support too!
ca. 2000
Botswana Offset 59,5 × 42

129 Ministerium für Gesundheit
Wir Aids? Nein, das ist nicht unser
Fall. Aber unsere Kinder und
unsere Enkelkinder sind nicht davor geschützt. Wenn sie sich
das Virus holen würden, würden
wir sie jedoch nicht im Stich
lassen. Denn dann benötigen sie
unsere Unterstützung und Zuneigung noch stärker. Und Sie,
wie verhalten Sie sich gegenüber
einer Person mit Aids? Aids
betrifft uns alle. Gehen Sie auf
Nummer sicher.
Got Aids, us? No we haven't. But
our children and our grandchildren are not safe from it. But if
they got the virus we wouldn't
leave them in the lurch. Because
they'd need our support and
affection even more then. And you,
how do you treat a person with
Aids? Aids affects us all. Play safe.
ca. 1995
Luxemburg Offset 59,5 × 42

130 Ministry of Health, Aids / STD
Unit, Gaborone
Kommunale Heimpflege /

verschafft: Liebe, Hoffnung,
Akzeptanz / Heimpflege schützt
dich besser
Community home based care /
provides: love, hope and
acceptance / home care better
care
ca. 2000
Botswana Offset 59,5 × 42

131 Aids Control Programme,
Ministry of Health
Aids-Kranke brauchen deine
Liebe, Pflege und Unterstützung /
du kriegst kein Aids, indem du
dich für Aids-Kranke einsetzt
Aids patients need your love, care
and support / You cannot catch
Aids through caring for Aids
patients
ca. 2000
Uganda Lithografie 42 × 59

132 Creative Realisation, cR
Werbeagentur AG Basel
Jürg Schaub (A)
Hannes Huber (D)
Bundesamt für Gesundheit, BAG
Aids-Hilfe Schweiz
Iris ist HIV-positiv. Wir stehen
zu ihr!
Iris is HIV positive. We're standing
by her!
1991
Schweiz Offset 128 × 275

133 Ines De Nil (F)
Deutsche Aids-Hilfe e.V.
Aids hat ein Gesicht / Du bist
herausgefordert / Aids-Kranke
können nicht warten. Deine
Spende hilft, die Not zu lindern
Aids has a face / You are
challenged / Aids patients cannot
wait. Your contribution helps to
make the hardship easier to bear
ca. 1995
Deutschland Offset 68 × 48

134 Garbergs (D)
Volksgesundheitsinstitut,
Riksförbundet för sexuell
upplysning, RFSU, Riksförbundet
för sexuellt likaberättigande, RFSL
Sei ein Gummi-Held / Macht
der Liebe
Be a rubber hero / Love power
ca. 1993
Schweden Offset 50 × 70

135 Garbergs (D)
Volksgesundheitsinstitut,
Riksförbundet för sexuell
upplysning, RFSU, Riksförbundet
för sexuellt likaberättigande, RFSL
Mach Liebe, nicht Aids / Macht
der Liebe
Make love not Aids / Love power

ca. 1993
Schweden Offset 50 × 70

136 Albert Sword (F)
Auckland Community Outreach
Centre, Maori Youth Project
Te Waka Awhina Takataapui Tane,
Auckland
Wissen macht stark / wir sind
junge Maori, schwul und
Überlebende
Strength comes from knowing /
being young Maori, gay and
survivors
ca. 1994
Neuseeland Offset 59,5 × 42

DANK
Unser Dank geht an Thomas Hill
für die von ihm zusammenge-
tragene, von der Plakatsammlung
des Museums für Gestaltung
Zürich 1998 angekaufte Samm-
lung von Aids-Präventionsplakaten
und für wertvolle Informationen
zum Thema, an Andrew Doupe
von der UNAIDS Genf und an die
Aids Info Docu Schweiz für
hilfreiche Unterstützung an Hatim
Abbas-Penella, Nassor Ali, Audrey
Brown, Dusan Brozman, Familie
Doan-Pham-Van Het, Eva Eiden-
benz, Lek Etter, Rita Frommen-
wiler, Ursula Glunk, Sid Ahmed
Hammoushe, Sara Hunn, Jeep
Kirstein-Somthong, Richard Müller,
Abdulla M. Mzee, Yijay Kumar
Singh, Kan Tai-keung, Katharina
Thölen und Esther Wenger für
Übersetzungen und Übersetzungs-
vermittlung.
Für Plakatzusendungen geht
unser Dank an: Richard Frick,
Aleksander Schumov, die UNAIDS-
Organisationen aus Botswana,
China, Hongkong, Swaziland,
Togo, Tunesien und Uganda sowie
an Cécile Guarino vom franzö-
sischen Centre Régional d'Infor-
mation et de Prévention sur le
Sida (CRIPS).

THANKS
Our thanks go to Thomas Hill
for the collection of Aids prevention
posters that he compiled, pur-
chased by the Museum für Ge-
staltung Zürich's Poster Collection
in 1998, and for valuable infor-
mation on the subject, to Andrew
Doupe of UNAIDS Geneva and to
Aids Info Docu Schweiz for helpful
support, to Hatim Abbas-Penella,
Nassor Ali, Audrey Brown, Dusan
Brozman, the Doan-Pham-Van
Het family, Eva Eidenbenz, Lek
Etter, Rita Frommenwiler, Ursula
Glunk, Sid Ahmed Hammoushe,
Sara Hunn, Jeep Kirstein-Somthong, Richard Müller, Abdulla
M. Mzee, Yijay Kumar Singh, Kan
Tai-keung, Katharina Thölen
and Esther Wenger for translations
and for arranging translations.
Many thanks for supplying posters
to: Richard Frick, Aleksander
Schumov, the UNAIDS organi-
zations of Botswana, China, Hong
Kong, Swaziland, Togo, Tunisia
and Uganda and to Cécile Guarino
of the French Centre Régional
d'Information et de Prévention sur
le Sida (CRIPS).

Nigel Barley geboren 1947 in Kingston, Grossbritannien. Seit 1978 arbeitet er am British Museum, heute als Kustos in der Ethnographischen Abteilung. Seine ethnologischen Feldstudien unternahm er in Afrika, Indonesien und Grossbritannien. Er arbeitet für das Fernsehen und Radio und ist Verfasser von anthropologischen Studien, historischen Abhandlungen und Romanen. Seine jüngste Publikation, «White Rajah», ist die Biografie von James Brooke, dem Gründer des Staates Sarawak.

Nigel Barley was born in 1947 in Kingston, England. Since 1978 he has worked at the British Museum where he is now an Assistant Keeper in the Ethnography Department and has done fieldwork in Africa, Indonesia and Great Britain. As well as television and radio work, he has written everything from academic anthropology to history and novels. His most recent work is "White Rajah", a biography of James Brooke, founder of the state of Sarawak.

Bettina Richter Studium der Kunstgeschichte, Germanistik und Romanistik in Heidelberg, Paris und Zürich. 1996 Promotion in Kunstgeschichte mit einer Arbeit über die Grafiken von Théophile-Alexandre Steinlen zum Ersten Weltkrieg. Seit 1997 wissenschaftliche Mitarbeiterin in der Plakatsammlung des Museums für Gestaltung Zürich.

Bettina Richter Studied art history, German and French in Heidelberg, Paris and Zurich. 1996 doctorate in art history with a thesis on the graphics based on the First World War by Théophile-Alexandre Steinlein. Scientific collabrator in the Museum für Gestaltung Zurich Poster Collection since 1997.

Ausgewählte Bibliografie / Bibliography (Selection)

Aids Info Doku Schweiz (Hg.), *Aids-Welten, Zwischen Resignation und Hoffnung,* Bern 1998.
Artis (Hg.), *Images pour la lutte contre le sida,* Paris 1993.
Bestmann, Anja / Reinhild Schumacher / Susanne Wünsch (Hg.), *Aids – weltweit und dichtdran,* Saarbrücken 1997.
Beule, Jürgen, *Bildwelten zu Aids: Die Immunschwäche im Spiegel der Printmedien,* Frankfurt a. Main 1999.
Dressler, Stefan / Klaus Michael Beier (Hg.), *Aids und Ethik,* Berlin 1994.
Gilman, Sander Lawrence, *Disease and representation: Images of illness from madness to Aids,* Ithaka 1988.
Gott, Ted (Hg.), *Don't leave me this way – Art in the age of Aids,* Canberra 1994.
Hausser, Dominique, *Psychosoziale und kulturelle Aspekte von Aids,* Bern 1994.
Kunstverein Hamburg (Hg.), *Gegendarstellung – Ethik und Ästhetik im Zeitalter von Aids,* Ausstellungskatalog, Hamburg 1992.
Meyer, Richard, "This is to enrage you: Gran Fury and the graphics of Aids Activism", in: Nina Felshin (Hg.), *But is it art? The spirit of art as activism,* Washington 1995.
Rigby, Hugh / Susan Leibtag (Hg.), *HardWear, The Art of Prevention,* Quon Editions, Hongkong 1994.
STOP AIDS-Kampagne der Aids-Hilfe Schweiz (AHS) und des Bundesamtes für Gesundheitswesen (BAG) (Hg.), *STOP AIDS, Die Stop Aids-Story 1987–1992,* Bern 1993.
Wegenstein, Bernadette, *Die Darstellung von Aids in den Medien,* Wien 1998.

«Poster Collection»
Herausgegeben von / Published by
Felix Studinka
Kurator der Plakatsammlung
Curator of the Poster Collection
Museum für Gestaltung Zürich
In Zusammenarbeit mit / in cooperation with
Bettina Richter, Wissenschaftliche Mitarbeiterin /
Scientific collaborator
Christina Reble, Publikationen / Publications
Museum für Gestaltung Zürich

Visuelle Strategien gegen Aids
Visual Strategies against Aids
Konzept und Redaktion / Concept and Editing:
Bettina Richter
Lektorat / Sub-editing: Karin Schneuwly
Übersetzung / Translation: Michael Robinson,
Wolfgang Himmelberg
Gestaltung / Design:
Integral Lars Müller / Hendrik Schwantes
Assistenz / Assistance: Christina Luzzi
Lithografie / Repro: Seelitho AG, CH-Gossau
Druck / Printing: Grafiche Duegi, I-Verona
Einband / Binding: Grafiche Duegi, I-Verona

© 2002
Museum für Gestaltung Zürich & Lars Müller Publishers

Museum für Gestaltung Zürich
Plakatsammlung / Poster Collection
Limmatstrasse 57
CH-8005 Zürich / Switzerland
e-mail: plakat.sammlung@museum-gestaltung.ch
http://www.museum-gestaltung.ch

Lars Müller Publishers
CH-5401 Baden / Switzerland
e-mail: books@lars-muller.ch
http://www.lars-muller-publishers.com

ISBN 3-907078-90-X
Erste Auflage / First Edition 2002

Printed in Italy

APG
Allgemeine Plakatgesellschaft